MANCHESTER UNITED'S
FIRST CHAMPIONSHIP

MANCHESTER UNITED'S FIRST CHAMPIONSHIP

The story of Manchester United's first title success in 1907–08

MARK METCALF

ACKNOWLEDGEMENTS

I would like to thank: D avid Wood, Paul Joannou, Steve Gordos, Paul Days, Peter Holme of the National Football Museum, Gordon Taylor, John Brompton and John Harvey. I would also like to the thank the staff at Bolton, Manchester and Sheffield Local Studies Libraries and all the staff at Derby Books.

First published in Great Britain in 2010 by The Derby Books Publishing Company Limited, 3 The Parker Centre, Derby, DE21 4SZ.

ISBN 978-1-85983-792-4

Printed and bound by Melita Press, Malta.

CONTENTS

FOREWORD

This is a match-by-match account of the season which proved a forerunner to many subsequent titles and trophies for Manchester United. Not only were these players responsible for making history for Manchester United, but the backbone of that team – with stars such as Billy Meredith and Charlie Roberts and the rebellious Sandy Turnbull – were instrumental in supporting Meredith to establish the Players' Union after initial efforts a few years previously had failed. Meredith felt the time had come to establish professional football as a recognised profession and to look to battle against the maximum wage, which was then set at £4, as well as many other restrictions, to the extent that quite a number of playing colleagues who had had to retire due to injury received no compensation whatsoever under the Workers' Compensation Act. These same players stayed out on strike prior to the 1909–10 season, inspite of many other players at other clubs returning to work when the Football Association refused to recognise the Union and was concerned that they also wished to join the General Federation of Trade Unions.

The famous picture of these players known as The Outcasts has pride of place in the PFA offices. The FA eventually caved in and the Union was recognised, and players of today will be forever in their debt.

Gordon Taylor
Chief Executive of the PFA

INTRODUCTION

Manchester United Football Club were formed in 1878 as Newton Heath (Lancashire and Yorkshire Railway) Football Club, entered the Football League in 1892 and at the start of the 1907–08 season had yet to win either the Division One title or the FA Cup. The club, after changing their name in April 1902, had won promotion back into Division One, after a 12-season absence, at the end of the 1905–06 season when they finished runners-up to Bristol City in Division Two. After having initially played home games at North Road, Newton Heath, by 1907 Bank Street, Clayton, was the club's home, although discussions about a move to the other side of the city were already underway.

Between September 1907 and April 1908 Manchester United thrilled their growing band of supporters, and by doing so provided the platform for the club's long-term success by racing to the Division One title for the first time in the club's history. In doing so they created what was then a League record of 52 points (there were two points for a win, one for a draw) in a League of 20 teams, winning 10 League games in a row between September and November 1907, including beating the then League champions Newcastle United 6–1 away. Subsequently, by beating QPR 4–0 in a replay at the start of the following season, Manchester United were the inaugural winners of the FA Charity Shield. The Manchester United side was managed by Ernest Mangnall, arguably the club's greatest ever manager.

GETTING STARTED

Manchester United had finished the 1906–07 season in eighth place in Division One, with 42 points from 38 games. This was nine behind the winners and victors for the second time in three years, Newcastle United. Confidence must have been high among the players, however, as statistics showed that following the team's reshuffle, starting against Aston Villa on New Year's Day 1907, Manchester United had improved immensely to capture 24 points from 17 matches to rise up the table from 15th place. In comparison, during the same period Newcastle had played 18 games and taken 23 points.

The key to the improvements in the club's fortunes had, ironically, come at Hyde Road, the then home of rivals Manchester City. Having been relegated from the First Division at the end of the 1901–02 season, joining Newton Heath in Division Two, City, under the direction of manager Tom Maley, forged their way back up the following season. Then, in 1903–04 City captured the FA Cup by beating Bolton in the Final, and they might even have done the double of League and Cup, finishing second to 'The Wednesday' in the race for the League title. Such rapid improvement had not gone unnoticed, but when the Football Association (FA) undertook an enquiry into City's rapid upturn in fortunes they found only some minor irregularities. However, things came to a head at the end of the following season when only a last-day defeat at Aston Villa denied City the title. Afterwards Alec Leake, the Villa captain, complained that City's outside-right Billy Meredith had offered him £10 to throw the game.

Meredith was found guilty of this offence by the FA and was fined and suspended from playing football for a year. Manchester City refused to provide financial help for him and so he decided to go public about what really was going on at the club, saying: 'What was the secret of the success of the Manchester City team? In my opinion, the fact that the club put aside the rule that no player should receive more than £4 a week. The team delivered the goods, the club paid for the goods delivered and both sides were satisfied.'

Such a statement indicating that Manchester City had broken the rule by which players wages were restricted to £4 a week was bound to alert the FA, who once again were forced to carry out an investigation into the financial activities of Manchester City. Maley was interviewed and he admitted that he had followed what seemed like standard English practice by making additional payments to all his players. He claimed that if all First Division clubs were investigated, not four would come out 'scatheless'.

As a result of their investigation, the FA suspended Tom Maley from football for life. Seventeen players were fined and suspended until January 1907. One of them, Billy Gillespie, the centre-forward at the 1904 FA Cup Final, even refused to pay his fine and instead emigrated to the United States, where he died in 1942.

With five directors also resigning, Manchester City placed the offending players up for sale, and at an auction at the Queen's Hotel in Manchester the Manchester United manager Ernest Mangnall signed Billy Meredith for just £500. While at City he had scored 145 goals in 338 games, so this was something of a bargain to put it mildly. Mangnall also purchased three other talented members of the City side: Herbert Burgess, Alex 'Sandy' Turnbull and Jimmy Bannister.

Mangnall had outwitted his rivals by arranging the deals with Manchester City in advance, but United already had a relationship with Meredith by dint of the fact that the money he had obtained to set up his sports equipment shop in St Peter's Square in the city had come from John Henry Davies, the Manchester United chairman. Whether that helped, no one can be absolutely certain, but it probably did. It is arguable that no Manchester United manager ever did better business than when Ernest Mangnall signed four Manchester City players at the end of 1906, all of whom made their debuts on New Year's Day 1907.

Mangnall had been appointed to the post of United manager – or secretary, as the post was then called – on 30 September 1903, replacing Jim West on the recommendation of Manchester United director and Football League president J.J. Bentley. Less than 18 months earlier the club had been on the brink of going out of business with debts of £2,670, only to be saved at the last minute when five local businessmen, including John Henry Davies, came forward to take over the club's debts.

It was Davies who provided Mangnall with the resources to seek out players good enough to take Manchester United back into Division One, a task made even more urgent by Manchester City's promotion at the end of the 1902–03 season.

Although Bolton-born Mangnall was able, in his first year, to bring in what proved to be three mainstays of the 1907–08 title-winning side in Harry Moger, Ernie Roberts and Dick Duckworth, gaining promotion did not come easily and Manchester United twice finished third, in 1903–04 and 1904–05, before achieving promotion in 1905–06.

Having initially struggled, the side's fine form in the second half of the 1906–07 season meant that Ernest Mangnall's movements in the transfer market during the close season were mainly designed to boost his reserve forces, but United did sign James Turnbull from Southern League side Leyton in May for what was described as a 'heavy fee' in the papers, while Bob Bonthron, after 134 first-team appearances, had moved on to Sunderland after losing his regular place in the side to Dick Holden towards the end of the previous campaign.

Ernest Mangnall's 1907 Summer Transfer Dealings:

In:

Herbert Broomfield (goalkeeper), Bolton Wanderers

George Stacey (full-back), Barnsley

Jimmy (James) Turnbull (forward), Leyton FC

Kerr Whiteside (half-back), Irvine Victoria

Tom Wilcox (goalkeeper), Blackpool

Also arriving were the following, none of whom ever made a first-team appearance:

P. McLarney, Norwich City

Mills, Willenhall Pickwick, Walsall

Handcock (forward), Hyde

Routledge (forward), Hooley Hill

Out – including total appearances and goals scored for Manchester United:

Tommy Blackstock (full-back), died (34/0)

Bob Bonthron (full-back), Sunderland (134/3)

Frank Buckley★ (half-back), Aston Villa (3/0)

Vince Hayes (full-back), Brentford – later returned (128/2)

Alexander 'Sandy' Robertson (forward), Bradford (34/10)

Charlie Sagar (forward), Atherton FC (33/24)

Alexander Robertson, unknown (35/1)

Bob Valentine (goalkeeper), Swinton RLFC (10/0)

Tommy Arkesden, Gainsborough Trinity (79/33)

Clem Beddow (forward), Burnley (34/15)

Joe Williams (forward), Unknown (3/1)

Alf Schofield (forward), retired (179/35)

★ Franklin Charles Buckley is better known as Major Frank Buckley following his World War One exploits. He later became a famous manager, with spells in charge at Norwich, Blackpool, Wolverhampton Wanderers, Notts County, Hull City, Leeds United and Walsall.

There was an unusual start to the season for some of the United players when they twice lined up against Bolton Wanderers over the first weekend in August to play the American game of pushball. Never before seen in Britain, this attracted a large crowd on the Saturday at the Royal Lancashire Show just outside Bolton to see both teams attempt to push a ball weighing 56 pounds, or 4st, into each other's goal. There was laughter when the ball rolled over the players, with both matches finishing in a draw at 1–1 and 2–2. The papers predicted the game was unlikely to catch on in Britain!

In the event, the United players must have heaved a sigh of relief when the first Reds-Whites practice match on a bright sunny day took place on Saturday 17 August.

Reds

Team: Moger, Holden, Burgess, Duckworth, Roberts, Bell, Berry, Picken, Menzies, Mills, H. Williams.

Whites

Team: Broomfield, McLarney, Stacey, Downie, Thomson, McGillivray, Meredith, Bannister, J. Turnbull, Dyer, Wall.

The good gate that attended the match meant a number of charities benefitted, and those who had made the effort to get to Bank Street not only got the chance to see James Turnbull in a United shirt for the first time, but also goalkeeper Herbert Broomfield, who had signed at the very end of the previous season from Bolton Wanderers. As Thomas Walter Wilcox, another 'keeper, had been signed from Blackpool after 37 League games in the Second Division the previous season, it was clear that United would be well served between the posts in the forthcoming campaign.

Another debutant was George Stacey, signed for £200 from Barnsley to understudy Herbert Burgess at left-back, but who was to go on to have a fine first season at United. P. McLarney, playing at right-back for the Whites, had arrived from Norwich City in the expectation it would take him a while to challenge for a first-team place – in fact he never did make an appearance in the first XI. Mills of Willenhall Pickwick, Walsall, was another who also never made the first team, and the same was true of two junior inside-forwards signed during the summer: Handcock from

Hyde and Routledge of Hooley Hill. All in all it meant that when the season began United had 31 professionals on their books. In the event the Whites won the first practice match 4–3, James Dyer opening the scoring and Wall scoring the second before Menzies and Williams levelled the scores at 2–2 at half-time.

Playing for the Reds, Alex Menzies was the man most likely to make way for James Turnbull in the first team after being singled out in the previous season's match reports as the weak link in the United five-man forward line.

Manchester United were due to start the season with an away fixture against Aston Villa. The side had lost 2–0 at Villa Park in the final away fixture of 1906. As this was prior to the signing of the Manchester City players the result would provide a good indication of how the side might fare in the coming season. Aston Villa had last won the First Division title at the end of the 1899–1900 season, their fifth success making them the most successful side ever at this time.

PEN PROFILES

Players who performed in the Manchester United first team during the 1907–08 season.

Goalkeepers

Harry Moger: had moved to United in May 1903 from Southampton, FA Cup finalists in 1900 and 1902, after finding his opportunities restricted by England international Jack Robinson. Although it took him until the start of the 1904–05 season before he became the regular between the United posts, his ever-increasing confidence over the intervening years meant he began the 1907–08 season assured of his place in the side.

Herbert Broomfield: signed from Bolton at the end of the previous season, but with Moger in fine form was to find his first-team opportunities restricted, and he was forced to wait until March 1908 before making his debut.

Full-backs

Dick Holden: had signed for United in May 1904 and made his debut against Blackpool the following April. When regular full-back Bob Bonthron had been injured the following season, Holden had taken the chance to make the position his own.

Herbert Burgess: one of four Manchester City players signed by Ernest Mangnall in December 1906 after winning the FA Cup in 1904 when Billy Meredith's single goal had been enough to overcome Bolton Wanderers in the Final. Although he was only 5ft 5in tall, he more than made up for his lack of height with his pace and surprising upper body strength. At the start of the 1907–08 season Burgess had played four times for England.

George Stacey: signed from Barnsley in the summer of 1907 at a reported fee of £200, he was to go on and have a long career at the club. By the time he finished playing, a career shortened by World War One had seen him make 267 first-team appearances. Nicknamed 'Silent' because he was a man of few words, Stacey did his talking on the pitch.

Ted Dalton: played his only ever match for United at Anfield in March 1908 when in a remarkable game Liverpool won 7–4.

Aaron Hulme: signed from Oldham Athletic in May 1906, the Manchester-born full-back was to make only one appearance against Preston North End on the final day of the League season. He later moved on to Nelson at the end of the following season after playing just three more first-team games.

Half-backs

Richard 'Dick' Duckworth: Manchester born and bred, Duckworth became a half-back after agreeing to swap from his centre-forward position for a reserve-team derby match with Manchester City on Christmas Day 1903. However, it was not until he forced his way past Alex Downie during the 1906–07 season that Duckworth became a regular in the United side. Once established, he went on to play some marvellous matches and helped form a formidable half-back line up with Roberts and Bell.

Charlie Roberts: Darlington's most famous footballer cost United a reported fee of £600, a huge sum at the time, to sign him from Grimsby at the end of the 1903–04 season. It was to prove money well spent. Roberts was to play some magnificent games at centre-half from where his tackling, passing and pace, added to his captaining skills, made him into one of the club's all-time greats. The fact that he was capped only three times by England can only be accounted for by the fact that Roberts was one of staunchest supporters of the fledgling Players' Union.

Alex Bell: born in South Africa to Scottish parents, Bell cost United £700 when he was signed, originally as a centre-forward, from Ayr Parkhouse in January 1903. Pushed into action at half-back, he soon turned the left-half position into his own from where he was quietly effective. After winning two League titles with United and an FA Cup-winners' medal, he later won the League title with Blackburn Rovers at the end of the 1913–14 season. Bell was awarded just a single cap for Scotland.

Ernest Thomson: signed from Darwen in May 1906, Thomson was to find his first-team path blocked by the Duckworth, Roberts and Bell half-back line up that provided United's backbone. He made his debut at Middlesbrough in September 1907, but by the time he moved on to Nelson in 1909 he had made only three further first-team appearances.

John McGillivray: was unfortunate to be cast in the role of understudy to Charlie Roberts. McGillivray's first-team debut was to come against

Blackpool in the FA Cup in January 1908, and he made his first of just three United League appearances the following weekend in a 2–0 defeat at Sheffield United. He was to move on to Southport Central in 1910.

Kerr Whiteside: made his only United appearance at Sheffield United in January 1908 and was to leave the club three years later to join Hurst, with whom he enjoyed a long association.

Alex Downie: by now in his 30s, Downie had joined Manchester United from Swindon Town in October 1902 and had been a regular in the side until 1906–07 when Duckworth had replaced him at right-half. He was to enjoy a well-earned benefit match in February 1908 and by the time he left the club in the summer of 1909 he was only nine matches short of 200 first-team appearances for United.

Forwards

Billy Meredith: one of the all-time greatest footballers, who would have been a star in whatever era he played. Manchester City signed him from Northwich Victoria in 1894, beginning a 30-year association with Manchester that delighted supporters. Having helped City to the Second Division title, the Welshman was part of the side who beat Bolton Wanderers in the 1904 FA Cup Final, in which he scored the only goal of the game. His first spell with Manchester City came to an end in December 1906 when he and three other players transferred across the city to United. After collecting two Division One League-winners' medals, along with another FA Cup-winners' medal, Meredith moved back to play for City in 1921 and even appeared in an FA Cup semi-final three years later in his 50th year. Meredith won an incredible 48 caps for his country during a period when matches with the other home nations were the staple fare.

James Bannister: after winning a Second Division Championship medal in 1903 with Manchester City the Leyland-born forward missed out on an FA Cup Final appearance the following season. One of four players signed from City in December 1906, Bannister made his debut at home to Aston Villa on New Year's Day 1907, and during the 1907–08 season he missed only two games.

Alex Menzies: had won the Scottish Cup with Hearts in 1906 before moving south in November of the same year. Although he scored on his League debut he struggled to make an impact in front of goal, and when United signed James Turnbull his days were numbered.

George Wall: very fast, tricky with a wonderful knack of cutting inside and surprising 'keepers with his shooting, the outside-left was a match for any full-back, and during the 1907–08 season he performed with distinction. The Sunderland-born man was to have a fine career at Manchester United, winning two League and one FA Cup-winners' medals and making 316 first-team appearances, during which he notched 98 goals. Wall had made his international debut playing against Wales in March 1907 and was to go on and play five times for his country.

Alexander 'Sandy' Turnbull: another player signed from Manchester City in 1906 after winning the Second Division Championship in 1903 and the

FA Cup in 1904. Brilliant in the air, he was on the end of many of Meredith's accurate crosses and corners. Turnbull was to finish as United's top scorer in the 1907–08 season and later scored the Cup-winning goal in the 1909 Final against Bristol City. After joining the Footballers' Battalion he was killed on active service in France on 3 May 1917.

James Turnbull: arrived at Bank Street in the summer of 1907 after scoring 15 goals for Leyton in the Southern League the previous season. After replacing Alex Menzies at centre-forward he was to go on to forge a lethal partnership with his namesake 'Sandy' Turnbull during the 1907–08 season.

William Berry: Sunderland-born, he had joined Manchester United in November 1906 from Southern League side Tottenham Hotspur as the club awaited the arrival of Billy Meredith, signed in May 1906 but unavailable until 1 January 1907. He had made nine appearances during the 1906–07 season but was to play only three times during the 1907–08 season.

Jack Picken: the Scotsman had scored on his League debut at home to Bristol City in September 1905, a season in which he was to finish as the club's leading scorer with 30 goals as United won promotion to Division One as runners-up to Bristol City. Having found goals much more difficult to come by in Division One, Picken was to enjoy few opportunities during the 1907–08 season but was to later play enough games during the 1910–11 season to qualify for a League Championship medal when United captured the title for a second time.

Tommy Wilson: the well-travelled Preston-born forward made his only Manchester United appearance against Blackburn Rovers at home in February 1908. He was to manage Rochdale after the war.

Harold Halse: only signed for Manchester United in March 1908, with Southend United, for whom he had scored 200 goals, receiving £350 for his services. He later made a goalscoring debut against Wednesday. He gained an FA Cup-winners' medal with United in 1909 and did the same with Aston Villa in 1913 before also playing in the FA Cup Final for a third side, Chelsea, in 1915, the Londoners losing out to Sheffield United 3–0 at Old Trafford.

Harry Williams: made only one appearance in 1907–08. Signed from Burnley in July 1903, he played 36 times in the Manchester United first team, scoring eight goals.

The Secretary / Manager

James Ernest Mangnall: was a surprise choice when he was appointed as Manchester United's secretary/manager in the autumn of 1903 as he had been the club secretary at Bolton in their 1898–99 relegation season and later secretary/manager at Burnley when the Turf Moor side were relegated in the following campaign. Mangnall's integrity had also been questioned when the Burnley 'keeper Jack Hillman had been found guilty of trying to bribe Nottingham Forest players to lose the last game of the season to help his side avoid relegation, for which the custodian was banned for a year. Mangnall was known to preach a gospel of physical fitness and team spirit and was typical of most English League managers up until the 1970s who believed that players should see relatively little of the ball during the week, and especially at the start of it, in order that they would be hungry for it on Saturdays. As he also had no previous reputation prior to 1903 for getting his sides to play good football there was little to suggest he would prove a success at Manchester United. But a success he was, going on to take the side back up into Division One, where he oversaw two League title triumphs, an FA Cup success and two Charity Shield triumphs before he decided to move to Manchester City.

Football in 1907

Football in 1907 was very different to today. Firstly there were no substitutes, so if a player got injured he was usually required to limp out the remainder of the match on the wing. There was also no such thing as advertising on strips, and numbering on shirts was a good 30 years away.

The ball used was rock hard and when it got wet it could become a very heavy object that also went out of shape. Pitches in the winter were often mud baths and became solid in the spring when the sun dried them out. Players' boots had studs hammered into the soles.

Initially, team formations had been entirely devoted to attack, with just two defenders and eight forwards, the aim being to rush forward with the ball, with individualism the key. While it is Scottish side Queen's Park who are believed to have been the first side to have recognised the value of 'letting the ball do the work', it is Preston North End, as winners of the first two Division One Championships in 1889 and 1890, who are credited with inventing the passing game.

This brought with it the need to adopt team formations for both attack and defence, leading to the 2-3-5 set up of two full-backs, three half-backs and five forwards then in place in 1907. The key player in this was the centre-half, who would be expected to surge forward in support of his forwards. It was usual for most sides to play their best most creative player in this key position. It was to be 1925 before the role of the centre-half changed when the offside law was altered so that players could now be onside if there were only two players between themselves and their opponents' goals rather than three.

One other significant difference compared with today is that in 1907 goalkeepers were allowed to handle the ball anywhere in their own half. If that might have made it easier for the men between the sticks, what did not was the law that allowed them to be shoulder-charged, just like any other player, with or without the ball.

At the start of the 1907–08 season Newcastle United were the reigning League champions, Nottingham Forest and Chelsea had replaced Derby County and Stoke City in Division One and The (Sheffield) Wednesday were the FA Cup holders.

THE 1907–08 CAMPAIGN

League Match 1

Against: Aston Villa (Away)

Date: Monday 2 September 1907

Attendance: 20,000

Result: Manchester United 4, Aston Villa 1

Aston Villa ⚽

Team: Cooch, Miles, Riley, J. Logan, Buckley, Codling, Wallace, Chapple, Hampton, Bache, Hall.

Scorer: Hampton

Manchester United ⚽⚽⚽⚽

Team: Moger, Holden, Burgess, Duckworth, Roberts, Bell, Meredith, Bannister, Menzies, A. Turnbull, Wall.

Scorers: Wall, Meredith (2), Bannister

Almost from the moment the game kicked-off Manchester United laid down a marker that they were going to be serious challengers for the First Division title. Quite simply Ernest Mangnall's side were much too good for a Villa side who were expected to challenge for the title themselves, with *The Manchester Courier* headline summing it up perfectly: 'Manchester United in brilliant form'. The report said that 'by defeating the Villa by four goals to one, United accomplished one of the best performances since the club was formed.'

It took only four minutes for the away team to take the lead through Wall, who received the ball from Bannister before beating the 'keeper from just inside the penalty area, after which Manchester United totally dominated the Birmingham side.

It was something of a miracle that as half-time approached the score remained just a single goal to United, with Sandy Turnbull having a header disallowed for offside. However, when Villa's right-half Chris Buckley suffered the misfortune of breaking his ankle, the reduction of the home side to just 10 men was simply too much and Meredith scored almost immediately to make it 2–0.

It was Meredith who scored the third goal, converting Wall's accurate cross, as the visitors continued to have all the serious play. Turnbull then had another effort disallowed for offside before Villa reduced the arrears with 10 minutes of the match remaining. Roberts was adjudged to have handled the ball and Joseph 'Harry' Hampton, scorer of both Villa's goals at the 1904–05 FA Cup Final when Newcastle United were beaten, scored from the resulting penalty. A strong, forceful, determined player, Hampton was the idol of the Villa Park faithful and formed a lethal partnership with Joe Bache.

Roused by conceding a goal, even to a great player such as Hampton, Manchester United pressed forward and Bannister pushed the ball home on 88 minutes to give the scoreline a more accurate reflection, of Aston Villa 1 Manchester United 4.

The Manchester Courier was full of praise for the whole team but singled out Roberts for particular praise while reporting that 'the 18,000 people who saw the game gave the Manchester men a capital reception as they left the field.'

A brilliant half-back line

'Mancunian', in the *Cricket and Football Field*, wrote: 'That our halves were brilliant is proved by the complete failure of the opposing front rank, and anything better than the play of Duckworth-Roberts-Bell – it would not be fair to divide them – would be hard to find.'

Manchester United had laid down a marker for the rest of the season – could they maintain it?

League Match 2

Against: Liverpool (Home)

Date: Saturday 7 September 1907

Attendance: 24,000

Result: Liverpool 0, Manchester United 4

Referee: C.C. Fallowfield of London.

Manchester United   ✪✪✪✪

Team: Moger, Holden, Burgess, Duckworth, Roberts, Bell, Meredith, Bannister, Menzies, A. Turnbull, Wall.

Scorers: A. Turnbull (3), Wall

Liverpool

Team: Hardy, Saul, West, Parry, Latham, Bradley, Goddard, C. Hewitt, J. Hewitt, Bowyer, Cox.

Following the opening-day success there was a good crowd of 24,000 for the first home game of the season against near neighbours Liverpool, who back at the end of the 1893–94 season had beaten the then Newton

Heath 2–0 at Ewood Park in the Football League Test match to take the Manchester side's place in Division One. Unlike Manchester United, Liverpool had already tasted success in the top flight with two Championship successes – in the 1900–01 and 1905–06 seasons. Liverpool had started the season in disappointing fashion having lost 3–1 away to Nottingham Forest in the first game.

The game took place at Bank Street, Clayton. This was Newton Heath/Manchester United's second ground and they occupied it from June 1893 until they moved to Old Trafford in February 1910. By 1907 Bank Street had undergone considerable improvements so that its capacity had risen to 50,000, although only 5,000 watched the final First Division fixture there on 22 January 1910. The ground was typical of Football League grounds of its time, being set among densely-populated working-class terraced housing, from which no doubt many of the club's supporters would have been drawn, and close to smoky factories.

The Bank Street pitch itself was nothing like the fabulous billiard table-like surfaces of the Premier League today and had little grass on it, especially in the winter. At the same time periods of heavy rain often meant there were mud patches and puddles for the players to overcome. The site is now occupied by the car park of the Manchester Velodrome, with a plaque on a house wall indicating the presence of the former ground.

United's second consecutive four goals in a match saw them thrash Liverpool. Afterwards *The Manchester Courier's* verdict was: 'Opinion was freely expressed by such judges of the game that no honour is too high for the team to achieve. Certainly the way in which the players have acquitted themselves so far leads one to expect great things from them this season.'

In the circumstances the Liverpool side did well to hold the hosts until Alex 'Sandy' Turnbull scored his first goal of the season with a right-footed shot on 33 minutes. After that it was simply a matter of how many Manchester United would get, and it would have been a lot more than four if the Liverpool side had not contained such a fine 'keeper as Sam Hardy. Born in Chesterfield, he had played for his home team before being signed in May 1905 by the Anfield side. He was to become a major star, bagging a League-winners' medal at the end of his first season. Hardy had gained the first of his 21 England caps earlier in the year when he was in the side that beat Ireland 1–0 at Goodison Park in February. He is rightly regarded as one of the finest 'keepers of all time.

The visitors had lost two key players in William McPherson and Alec Raisbeck, with the reshuffle seeing Charlie Hewitt and Sam Bowyer moved to inside-right and left respectively, but even with 13 men it was unlikely Liverpool could have done much to contain a United side in rampant form.

The Manchester Courier reported Duckworth afterwards as being the best half on the field and giving great support to Meredith. Moger, Burgess and Holden completely blanked out the Liverpool forwards and the paper felt it 'would take a very clever set of forwards to score many goals against United.'

The loud cheers for both groups of players when they emerged from the tunnel at the start was an indication of a healthy away support. When Roberts won the toss he chose to kick with the breeze, and Menzies headed narrowly wide in the first minute. Hardy then produced a brilliant save to deny Sandy Turnbull, whose header from a Billy Meredith cross seemed certain to open the scoring; however, the 'keeper was powerless to prevent the same players combining for the first goal. Wall scored the second just before the break after Turnbull's run had split the Liverpool defence, and when he pulled the ball back the United outside-left hit a sweet half-volley. In the second half Turnbull, with two headers, both from Wall's corners, completed his hat-trick.

This was a very fine performance, which gave Manchester United a goal average of eight goals to one with maximum points to take the club to the top of the League. It was going to take a very good side indeed to knock them off it. The result saw Liverpool occupy bottom spot with no points from their opening two games. Hardy's expertise was going to be needed!

George Latham

The Liverpool centre-half had been a member of the famous Welsh team who had won the Home International Championships for the first time the previous season, thus breaking Scotland and England's monopoly. The side, which also contained Billy Meredith as well as his brother Sam, beat Ireland 3–2 away and Scotland 1–0 at home before holding England 1–1 to finish at the top of the table. A crowd of 22,000 watched the final match at Craven Cottage.

League Match 3

Against: Middlesbrough (Home)

Date: Monday 9 September 1907

Result: Manchester United 2, Middlesbrough 1

Manchester United   ⚽ ⚽

Team: Moger, Holden, Burgess, Duckworth, Roberts, Bell, Meredith, Bannister, Menzies, A. Turnbull, Wall.

Scorer: A. Turnbull (2)

Middlesbrough   ⚽

Team: Williamson, Brown, Watson, S. Aitken, A. Aitken, Harkins, Brawn, Bloomer, Common, Wilcox, Roberts.

Scorer: Wilcox

The third game of the season brought Middlesbrough to Bank Street. Like United they had won their first two matches of the season, beating Birmingham 1–0 at home and Nottingham Forest 3–0 away.

With Bell recovering from the injury that had forced him to miss the last few minutes of the Liverpool game two days earlier, the home side were able to field the same side for the third consecutive match.

With another 20,000-plus crowd in attendance there was a real expectation of a fine game in prospect. And so it proved, with both sides playing a whole-hearted game, and although Manchester United deserved to capture both points by the end of the game, Middlesbrough had shown they were themselves in for a fine season. Bill Brawn, in particular, constantly threatened the United rearguard with his charging runs down the wing and both Holden and Burgess had to play well to stop him as he swapped wings throughout.

It was the away side who were first to show, but Menzies brought the home side into the match with two drives, one of which smashed against the crossbar. Bannister should have done better but failed to keep his shot down. Fred Wilcox then allowed Moger to show his skills, the 'keeper pushing away a dangerous shot. Steve Bloomer could have then given Middlesbrough the lead but failed to hit the target when well placed. Wall, meanwhile, was finding it difficult to use his pace and skill to beat Sam Aitken and at half-time the match remained goalless.

How it remained so in the first few minutes after the restart was amazing, Wilcox somehow conspiring to head over from just a couple of yards out before at the other end Wall, escaping his marker's attention for once, hit a powerful shot that crashed back off the bar. Despite this misfortune it seemed to inspire the Manchester United side, and slowly but surely Middlesbrough were pushed back.

Tim Williamson in the Boro goal was in fine form but he could do nothing with a fast high drive by Turnbull for his fourth goal of the season. Ten minutes later the same player made it 2–0, but in truth he could not miss after Meredith tore down the wing, ran past the Boro defence and curled back a cross that his colleague simply had to get his head to for the ball to enter the net. Towards the end the away side got the goal their play deserved when Brawn's shot across the goal was turned in by Wilcox.

It had been a great game. Turnbull had been the outstanding player and *The Manchester Courier* felt it was surely only a matter of time before he was called-up to play for Scotland, stating that 'he cannot be left out if any consideration is given to him at all.' In fact, this outstanding player never did get the chance to represent his country. Born just outside Kilmarnock, he was, of course, to go on and score Manchester United's winning goal in the 1909 FA Cup Final with Bristol City. Victory over Middlesbrough maintained his side at the top of the First Division table after three games – there was a long way to go but it was clear that the side fashioned by Mangnall was in with a very good shout of winning the club's first major title. The first trophy won by Newton Heath had, in fact, been in 1886 when they beat Manchester FC to win the Manchester and District Challenge Cup.

Steve Bloomer – Derby County, Middlesbrough and England

Inside-right Bloomer would win a place in any best-ever Derby County side. A magnificent passer of the ball, he also possessed a powerful, accurate shot such that by the time he retired in 1914 at aged 40 he had rattled up 392 goals in 599 games for Derby and Middlesbrough, finishing as top scorer in the First Division on five occasions. During the 1894–95 season he scored twice on his England international debut in a 9–0 victory over Ireland. Then, on 16 March 1896 he became one of a select band of players to score five goals in an England shirt (George Hall and Malcolm MacDonald later became the others) as Wales were beaten 9–1 in Cardiff.

Bloomer was considered by Frederick Wall, the president of the Football Association, to be the best goalscorer he ever saw. He said: 'He was a great marksmen, and his splendid passes were generally made with one touch.' Bloomer, however, had an unfortunate record in FA Cup Finals, playing and losing in two, and was missing, out injured, when Derby crashed to a record 6–0 defeat to Bury at the 1903 Final.

Middlesbrough's best-ever 'keeper

Reginald Garnet 'Tim' Williamson is possibly the best goalkeeper Middlesbrough have ever had. He is the club's all-time record appearance holder with over 600 first-team appearances, of which a staggering 130 were consecutive. He became England's youngest capped 'keeper when he played against Ireland in February 1905 but during a quiet game he dropped the ball into his own net, and in addition to suffering the indignity of conceding an own-goal he ended up waiting another six years for a cap, with Sam Hardy's brilliance keeping him out of the side. Williamson was to subsequently make a total of seven international appearances. He was one of the first 'keepers to take penalties, scoring twice.

League Match 4

Against: Middlesbrough (Away)

Date: Saturday 14 September 1907

Attendance: 18,000

Result: Middlesbrough 2, Manchester United 1

Middlesbrough

Team: Williamson, Brown, Watson, S. Aitken, A. Aitken, Harkins, Brawn, Bloomer, Common, Wilcox, Roberts.

Scorers: Wilcox, S. Aitken

Manchester United

Team: Moger, Holden, Burgess, Duckworth, Roberts, Thomson, Meredith, Bannister, Menzies, A. Turnbull, Wall.

Scorer: Bannister

Following an indiscretion by Alf Common, which saw the centre-forward fined £10 and have the captaincy taken off him, Sam Aitken had been appointed Boro captain before the match. He celebrated by playing one of the games of his life, not only blotting out Menzies, but also having time to get forward to score.

With Bell ruled unfit to play, Ernest Thomson was selected to make his debut for United at left-half. Signed from Darwen at the end of the 1905–06 season, Thomson was to find first-team opportunities hard to come by during an era when United's half-back line up was arguably as strong as at any time in the club's history.

After a tentative opening spell the game came to life when Meredith's drive beat Williamson, only to flash behind off the top of the bar. The home crowd then screamed for a penalty when Roberts appeared to handle a John Harkins drive, before Brawn might have scored with a close-range header. Wilcox was then unlucky to see his header hit the bar but the Boro man was not to be denied on 35 minutes when, after beating Holden, he scored from close range.

A minute later Sam Aitken scored one of the best goals ever seen at Ayresome Park during its long history, firing an unstoppable shot from 40 yards past Moger to the enthusiasm of the crowd. Two goals down at half-time, United showed they were far from finished when Roberts skimmed the bar with a speculative effort before Williamson made a great save from Wall, the United outside-left's only real contribution in the 90 minutes.

Although Bannister did reduce the arrears with 15 minutes remaining, Middlesbrough were able to hang on and ensure a first defeat of the season for United in what had been a very fine match.

Top of the table

Team	Played	Points
Man Utd	4	6
Middlesbrough	4	6
Bury	4	6
The Wednesday	3	5

Alf Common

Played and scored for Sheffield United at the 1902 FA Cup Final that the Blades won after a replay, but he is best known for being the first player to be transferred for a fee of £1,000 when he moved from Sunderland to Middlesbrough in February 1905. Common played three games for England, scoring twice.

Middlesbrough Player-manager

Andy Aitken was the Middlesbrough player-manager. Signed from Newcastle, where he had won one League title and twice reached the FA Cup Final, Aitken was to play 14 times for Scotland, one of which included the match against England on 4 April 1908 at Hampden Park that attracted a then world record crowd of 121,452.

League Match 5

Against: Sheffield United (Home)

Date: Saturday 21 September 1907

Attendance: 25,000

Result: Manchester United 2, Sheffield United 1

Referee: A. Green of West Bromwich.

Manchester United ☹ ☹

Team: Moger, Holden, Burgess, Duckworth, Roberts, Bell, Meredith, Bannister, Menzies, A. Turnbull, Wall.

Scorer: A. Turnbull (2)

Sheffield United ☹

Team: Leivesley, Benson, C. Johnson, McGuire, B. Wilkinson, Needham, Thompson, Bluff, Brown, Levisk, Lipsham.

Scorer: Brown

The return of Bell at left-half in place of Thomson was the only change as United attempted to put the previous weekend's defeat at Middlesbrough behind them. Sheffield United arrived at Clayton undefeated with a win and two draws from their first three games. The Steel City club had taken the League title back in 1897–98, and having finished in fourth place at the end of 1906–07 they were regarded as one of the favourites for the title at the beginning of the following campaign.

The Sheffield United side contained one of the outstanding footballers of his generation in Ernest Needham. A left-half, he had joined the club in 1892 and two years later, after playing his part in the Blades' successful promotion push, gained his first of 16 England caps in which he scored three goals. Needham was the captain of the Sheffield United side that won the First Division in 1897–98 but had to accept a losers' medal when Spurs beat his team in the 1901 FA Cup Final after a replay. The following season, however, Needham enjoyed success in the Final when Sheffield United beat Southampton, again after a replay. Needham was also a fine cricketer and played for Derbyshire in the County Championship, scoring 6,550 runs before he retired in 1922.

The match was watched by a healthy crowd of 25,000 people and they witnessed a very tight game, which afterwards both *The Sheffield Independent* and *The Manchester Evening News* felt had left the away side unlucky not to gain a point. Sheffield were certainly unlucky when the referee Mr Green blew for a foul by Burgess on Arthur Brown as the home player's challenge had, in fact, failed to halt the Sheffield forward who was shaping to beat Moger.

That aside, Ernest Mangnall's side did by far the most attacking in a game in which, according to *The Sheffield Independent*, 'the half-back play was the most distinctive feature.' It added that for the home side 'Duckworth, Roberts and Bell had played a rare game.'

Turnbull's opening goal on eight minutes came after receiving the ball from Roberts. He swivelled to beat Joe Leivesley with a fierce right-foot shot. Sheffield equalised on 20 minutes when Burgess lost the ball and George Thompson broke away and centred for Brown, who held off two challenges before beating Moger. The away side were then grateful for the fine form of Leivesley in goal, who seemed determined to ensure his side made the short trip home with at least a point. He made some decisive catches when the United wingers crossed and also handled a series of hard drives from the edge of the box. The 'keeper could do nothing, however, to prevent Turnbull's deft touch from a Meredith cross before half-time that ultimately won the game for the home side. With two goals it was not therefore surprising that both *The Manchester Evening News* and *The Sheffield Independent* selected Turnbull as the outstanding forward on the field, but Brown was rated not too far behind. In comparison, both papers felt that the home side's centre-forward Menzies had player poorly.

The victory was especially sweet for the chairman of Manchester United at the time, J.J. Bentley, who was celebrating his silver wedding anniversary that day.

Lancashire Senior Cup

Date: Monday 23 September 1907

Result: Manchester City 0, Manchester United 3

On Monday 23 September 1907 United easily beat Manchester City 3–0 in a game played at City's then ground, Hyde Road. Both sides were missing three regular first teamers for this latest game, which in United's case allowed James Turnbull to take Menzies's place in the following line up: Manchester United: Moger, Holden, Burgess, Duckworth, Roberts, Bell, William Berry, John Picken, J. Turnbull, A. Turnbull, Wall.

A crowd of 5,500 saw an early goal from Sandy Turnbull but the best was the second. Following a brilliant run, in which he eluded Eadie, James Turnbull beat Smith for a glorious goal to signal he was ready for a regular run in the United first team. Wall scored the third goal in the second half.

League Match 6

Against: Chelsea (Away)

Date: Saturday 28 September 1907

Result: Chelsea 1, Manchester United 4

Referee: J.G.A. Sharp of Lichfield.

Chelsea

Team: Whitley, Lyon, Mackie, Key, McRoberts, Proudfoot, Moran, Bridgeman, Hilsdon, Windridge, Fairgray.

Scorer: Hilsdon

Manchester United   ✪ ✪ ✪ ✪

Team: Moger, Holden, Burgess, Duckworth, Roberts, Bell, Meredith, Bannister, J. Turnbull, A. Turnbull, Wall.

Scorers: Meredith (2), A. Turnbull, Bannister

With The Wedneday having beaten Bristol City 5—3 in midweek, United went to Chelsea lying in second place in the table, a point behind the Yorkshire side.

Newly-promoted Chelsea had beaten League champions Newcastle United 2—0 just five days previously. The match against Manchester United was played on a boiling hot day in which temperatures reached 100F at one point.

The large crowd were treated to a magnificent display, sadly not by their own side, but that did not stop them appreciating the away side, whom they roundly applauded off the field at the end.

Having failed to hit the net in five games, and seen James Turnbull score a superb goal in the Monday match against Manchester City, Alex Menzies found himself replaced at centre-forward by the ex-Leyton man. On this showing the decision looked a wise one. The star of the show was again Meredith who was constantly fed the ball by Sandy Turnbull and Bannister. 'He certainly gave as good an exhibition of wing play as anyone could wish for,' reported *The Manchester Courier*. His second and United's fourth right at the end of the match was a sparking run and finish that brought the biggest and longest cheer of the match. There was also praise in *The Manchester Evening News* for Moger, who during the times when Chelsea put pressure on the United goal showed some confident handling of the ball. Bell also received praise but this was a fine team effort all round, leading the *Courier* reporter to end his match report with the following: 'The men, extremely capable individually, have developed into an extremely formidable side now that they have become thoroughly acquainted with each other's play.'

Ernest Mangnall's side had gone in front as early as the 10th minute, Chelsea foolishly leaving Meredith unattended to beat Bob Mackie and he hit a low drive that Jack Whitley was powerless to stop. The home side did manage to equalise when from a corner George Hilsdon headed past Moger, but a lovely drive from Sandy Turnbull restored the United lead, before, in the 48th minute, Bannister from just three yards out knocked a Wall cross into an unguarded net. The match was long over as a contest when Meredith scored in the last minute.

The victory took United back to the top of the table after The Wednesday lost a thrilling game at Hyde Road, Manchester City beating the FA Cup holders 3–2.

Top of the table

Team	Played	Points
Man Utd	6	10
Bury	7	10
The Wednesday	6	9
Everton	6	8

Jimmy Windridge

An inside-forward, Windridge scored more than 50 goals for Chelsea between 1905 and 1911 to earn himself eight England caps, in which he scored seven goals.

George Hilsdon

Hilsdon is currently Chelsea's eighth highest goalscorer of all time with 107 goals from 164 first-team appearances between 1906–12. He played eight England games, scoring 14 goals, eight of which came during England's first overseas tour at the end of the 1907–08 season.

Friendly

Date: Monday 30 September 1907

Result: Leyton 2, Manchester United 1

United travelled the short distance to play Southern League Leyton, a match arranged as part of the agreement that had seen James Turnbull move north during the summer. It was his striking partner, Sandy, who scored in a 2–1 defeat in a match which saw the famous English music hall comedian George Robey appear as a guest for United in their forward line. In 1909, Robey was hired by Manchester United to present the players with the kit specially made for the 1909 FA Cup Final, before providing the post-match entertainment after their 1–0 victory over Bristol City.

League Match 7

Against: Nottingham Forest (Home)

Date: Saturday 5 October 1907

Attendance: 20,000

Result: Manchester United 4, Nottingham Forest 0

Manchester United ✪ ✪ ✪ ✪

Team: Moger, Holden, Burgess, Duckworth, Roberts, Bell, Meredith, Bannister, J. Turnbull, A. Turnbull, Wall.

Scorers: Bannister, Wall, J. Turnbull, own-goal

Nottingham Forest

Team: Linacre, Dudley, Maltby, Hughes, Needham, Armstrong, Hooper, Marrison, Green, Morris, West.

Having won so superbly and easily the previous weekend there was no surprise when the same United side was selected to face the previous season's Division Two champions at home. Nottingham Forest were making their first appearance at Clayton since they opposed Newton Heath there in 1893. That match in September ended 1–1 to leave Heath on five points from their first four games of the season and in ninth place in the 16-team table. It was a decent start and augured well for a better season after Heath had only just avoided relegation at the end of the previous season by beating Small Heath (now Birmingham City) in the Test match Play-offs that had been introduced to decide promotion and relegation. Newton Heath had finished bottom of Division One with just 18 points from 30 games.

In fact, the 1893–94 season was a disaster, and following the draw with Forest, Heath went on a run where they won two and lost 14 of their next 16 League games. They finished bottom of the table and were again in the test matches. This time there was no reprieve as before 6,000 spectators at Ewood Park they lost 2–0 to Liverpool and were relegated.

It was to be 12 seasons before United emerged back into Division One just as Forest experienced the drop.

Although the home side again won convincingly, most of the crowd were left disappointed, as the Manchester side were unable to replicate their fine form of previous matches. What did not help was persistent rain, reducing the ground to a mud bath in patches, and a ball that looked out of shape. However, no side, no matter how good, can play at their best every week.

The away side had clearly earmarked Meredith as the man to watch and he was rarely left without two players close by. Rather than search the Welshman out the United players did the sensible thing and used the additional space left vacant by his watching defenders. For doing so, Duckworth and Bannister were criticised by the *Manchester Courier's* reporter. With Meredith so tightly marked much of the United attacking play was switched to the left, and Wall scored a good goal, the third of the match. There was also joy for home debutant Jimmy Turnbull, who got his first goal for the club by scoring the fourth, reward for a fine performance that drew praise from the reporter in *Athletic News*, who said 'Turnbull showed cleverness with the ball, was quick and shot with strength. He adds weight to the line and looks like keeping his place in the team.'

The home side had opened the scoring on just 10 minutes with a shot from 15 yards by Bannister, and although Forest rarely looked like drawing level there was relief when the second goal was recorded just after half-time. Jack Armstrong, the Forest left-half, totally mistimed his attempted clearance from the edge of the penalty area to send the ball flashing into his own goal.

Roberts was rated by reporters as the best player on show.

The result maintained United's lead at the top of the table on 12 points from seven games, one ahead of The Wednesday. Forest were in 15th place, five places and three points ahead of bottom-placed Chelsea.

Meredith's Welsh teammates

Forest's Arthur William Green and Grenville Morris were teammates of Billy Meredith in the famous Welsh side that had won the Home International Championship for the first time in 1907. Morris is Forest's all-time record goalscorer, with 199 in the League alone.

League Match 8 ——————————————

Against: Newcastle United (Away)

Date: Saturday 12 October 1907

Attendance: 25,000

Result: Newcastle United 1, Manchester United 6

Newcastle United

Team: Lawrence, McCombie, Carr, McWilliam, Veitch, Willis, Gardner, Speedie, Hall, Orr, G. Hedley.

Scorer: McWilliam

Manchester United

Team: Moger, Holden, Stacey (debut match), Duckworth, Roberts, Bell, Meredith, Bannister, J. Turnbull, A. Turnbull, Wall.

Scorers: Meredith, J. Turnbull, A. Turnbull, Wall (2), Roberts

This was at the time unarguably Manchester United's finest hour, or 90 minutes to be entirely accurate. Newcastle were the current League champions and had thrashed Manchester United at home in the previous season 5–0, as well as winning at Bank Street 3–1. The home side, it was true, had not started the current campaign in particularly good form, but before kick-off they were still not too far behind the League leaders in seventh place with just four points fewer.

Both sides included debutants, with George Hedley at outside-left for the home team and Manchester United's George Stacey at left-back replacing Burgess, who had been called upon to play at nearby Roker Park as part of the Football League side which that day beat the Irish League 6–3.

Heavy rain not only meant the ground at St James' Park was soft at the start, but had also reduced the size of the crowd, who saw Manchester United roar into a fourth-minute lead. Bannister and James Turnbull broke open the home defence and when the ball reached Meredith he drilled an accurate shot from the tightest of angles into the roof of the net. It was a remarkable goal, the 200th in the League for this brilliant player. Stung by going behind, the home side rallied and Moger was forced to make a diving save from Finlay Speedie to help United retain their lead.

Disaster struck Andy McCrombie on 25 minutes when he turned Meredith's cross into the path of James Turnbull, who made it 2–0. With the home defence now in disarray David Willis foolishly handled in the box soon after and Sandy Turnbull scored from the spot to make it 3–0. Hedley did his best to get a goal back but found Moger in fine form, and then Newcastle had to thank their 'keeper, Jimmy Lawrence, for preventing Wall making it 4–0 just before the break. Lawrence had twice played for Newcastle in the FA Cup Final, but he had finished with losers' medals on both occasions in 1905 and 1906 and was to suffer the same fate at the end of the 1907–08 season and in 1911. He did collect a winners' medal in 1910, however, when Newcastle beat Barnsley after a replay in the Final. Newcastle captain Colin Veitch and Jock Rutherford also achieved similar feats for the Geordies.

Five minutes into the second period any hopes the home fans might have entertained of a famous comeback had disappeared when Wall got the goal his play deserved, driving the ball past an unsighted Lawrence from the edge of the penalty area. The 'keeper had only to wait another minute to concede a fifth when Roberts, dashing forward, received a square ball from Meredith before advancing to smash the ball home from 20 yards. In an ideal world United's sixth would have been scored by Bannister so that all five forwards had scored, but instead it was Wall who made it 6–0 by sweeping home a Meredith cross with the home defence by now totally ragged. Near the very end of the game Peter McWilliam did manage to pull a goal back with a good shot after a dribbling run, but it was a well beaten – no, slaughtered – Newcastle side that ran off at the end.

Every United player had played magnificently and Newcastle had suffered their biggest ever home defeat at the time. Sunderland later beat them 9–1 during the 1908–09 season when remarkably Newcastle again won the League. Despite their obvious disappointment the huge crowd knew they had witnessed a remarkable performance, and at the end they cheered the away side off the pitch.

The Manchester Evening News reported: 'The Manchester triumph was the result of skill, and it is a long while since the defence of Lawrence, McCombie and Carr was so completely outwitted. The Manchester men are to be complimented upon a performance which will stand out as one of the achievements of the season.'

Colin Veitch

Newcastle-born Veitch made his debut at 19 before becoming a regular in the 1902–03 season. Generally regarded as a midfield player, he was also versatile enough to play in most other positions during his long career in a period when for much of the time the Magpies were England's number-one side, capturing the Football League Championship in the 1904–05, 1906–07 and 1908–09 seasons and the FA Cup in 1910.

Veitch was a leading figure in the Association Football Players' Union (AFPU) at a time when players were badly exploited, serving as the chairman until he retired from football on the outbreak of World War One. It is likely that Veitch would have won more than six caps for his country if it was not for his role in the Union as he was an astute reader of the game and a natural captain on and off the field. These qualities, combined with his versatility, would win him a place in any best-ever Newcastle line up.

Veitch was also a close friend of playwright George Bernard Shaw and a committed socialist.

Lancashire Senior Cup

Date: Monday 14 October 1907

Result: Manchester United 2, Bolton Wanderers 0

Berry replaced Meredith in the side that had faced Newcastle United in a game in which both James and Sandy Turnbull got a goal, the latter also missing a penalty.

New Signings

Ernest Mangnall signed David Christie for Hurlford FC and Joe Ford from Crewe Alexandra in October 1907. Both were forwards who went on to make two and five first-team United appearances respectively.

League Match 9

Against: Blackburn Rovers (Away)

Date: Saturday 19 October 1907

Result: Blackburn Rovers 1, Manchester United 5

Attendance: 27,400

Referee: R. Horrocks of Bolton.

Blackburn Rovers

Team: McIver, Crompton, Cowell, Wolstenholme, Manning, Bradshaw, Whittaker, Latheron, Martin, Davies, Bracegirdle.

Scorer: Davies

Manchester United

Team: Moger, Holden, Burgess, Duckworth, Roberts, Bell, Meredith, Bannister, J. Turnbull, A. Turnbull, Wall.

Scorers: A. Turnbull (3), J. Turnbull (2)

Having hammered the League champions Newcastle the previous weekend, United must have travelled with confidence to take on near neighbours Blackburn Rovers. Both sides were boosted by the return of key players, back after playing for the Football League against the Irish League at Roker Park. The Irish had taken a two-goal lead before losing 6–3.

Burgess's recall meant Stacey missed out on his second appearance – though his time would come – while Bob Crompton returned as the Rovers skipper. A right-back, Crompton was born in Blackburn and played throughout his career for the local team, ending up making 528 appearances, a figure shortened by World War One. Although solidly built, he was not typical of the bruising defenders of his time and was a master tactician.

He made his debut in 1897 as a 17-year-old, and five years later he was picked to play for England against Wales in the opening match of that season's Home Championship. It was to be the first of 41 caps for his country, a record that stood until well after World War Two. Considering that there were at the time only three regular international games per season then the modern equivalent would be well over 100 caps.

Crompton captained his country on 22 occasions. He was to win two League-winners' medals, in 1911–12 and at the end of the 1913–14 season. After retiring from playing he then managed Rovers as they won the FA Cup for a then record-equalling (with Aston Villa) sixth time by beating Huddersfield 3–1 at Wembley in 1928.

The Sunderland and Arsenal legend Charlie Buchan later wrote of Crompton that he was 'the finest footballer in the world before World War One.'

Crompton may have been a fine footballer but not even a man of his many talents could prevent a rampant United side thrashing his charges in October 1907. It may have been 5–1 but 10–1 would not have been an injustice, with the *Lancashire Evening Telegraph* (*L.E.T*) – which more than 100 years later still covers goings on across East Lancashire – saying of the away side: 'They are the most effective combination that has been seen on the Ewood Ground for a good many years. There may have been visitors more beautiful to behold, but I cannot recollect a team that backed up clever midfield play with such deadliness in front of goal.'

It was only the fifth time that Rovers had conceded five at home since they became one of the inaugural sides to join the Football League in 1888. The *L.E.T* added 'They were fairly and squarely beaten by an immensely superior team led by Meredith and Wall, who made ground all the time, and showed the crowd how the game should be played. The United have a fine, well-balanced team, and with the least bit of luck will win the Championship.' Rovers had been confident of winning before the match, having played and won all four previous home games without even conceding a goal.

The away side's crucial second goal that restored their lead was the pick of the bunch, Meredith showing pace and trickery to bamboozle the Blackburn backs before crossing to 'Sandy' Turnbull who, hurling himself forward, headed the ball from little more than a foot off the ground past Willie McIver in the Rovers goal. Wall was not to be outdone, however, and later, after leaving Crompton trailing in his wake, he whipped over a cross that gave Jimmy Turnbull the easiest of tasks to head into the net for United's fourth goal.

It had taken the away side just 10 minutes to open the scoring before a crowd of 27,400, Rovers' largest of the season, that paid a total of £897 for the privilege. On a ground made soft by heavy rain, Duckworth captured the ball near the halfway line and, after beating Arthur Cowell, ran down the wing before finding Sandy Turnbull, who drove the ball past the Rovers 'keeper.

Rovers equalised 10 minutes later when Bill 'Tinker' Davies curled the ball away from Moger but when United strode back into the lead with just five minutes of the first half remaining the knowledge that they would be playing with a strong breeze in the second half must have given Mangnall's men real confidence.

It was therefore no great surprise when Meredith teed Sandy Turnbull up for the third, and it was from another Meredith floated cross that the same man scored his third goal and the away side's fifth.

The Athletic News was to the point when it summed up the away side's performance: 'Manchester United were splendid everywhere' and 'the best feature was their half-back line up.' Roberts was singled out as the best player for the winning team who were now hot favourites to win the League.

Yet despite such a heavy defeat *The Athletic News* and perhaps less surprisingly the *L.E.T* both selected Crompton as the best player, with *The Athletic News* stating: 'His greatness was plain to see and I cannot help but wonder what would have happened if the England captain had not been playing for Rovers.'

League Match 10

Against: Bolton Wanderers (Home)

Date: Saturday 26 October 1907

Attendance: 35,000

Result: Manchester United 2, Bolton Wanderers 1

Manchester United

Team: Moger, Holden, Burgess, Duckworth, Roberts, Bell, Meredith, Bannister, J. Turnbull, A. Turnbull, Wall.

Scorers: A. Turnbull, J. Turnbull

Bolton Wanderers

Team: Edmondson, Slater, Stanley, Greenhaugh, Clifford, Boyd, Stokes, Owen, Shepherd, White, McEwan.

Scorer: Boyd

Knowing that their opponents had won five in a row, the Bolton manager John Somerville, who as a player was a member of the Trotters' defeated 1894 FA Cup Final side, adopted a cautious approach. His side were lying only one place and two points outside the relegation zone and a heavy defeat would have been damaging for morale following two successive victories against Chelsea and Nottingham Forest.

Wanderers were in the middle of a spell where they were too good for Division Two football but not good enough for the top flight, having gone down in 1898–99 and 1902–03 only to be promoted in 1899–1900 and 1904–05. They were to be relegated again at the end of the 1907–08 season, before returning as Division Two champions the following season, only to go down again in 1909–10 before returning once again in 1910–11. At least it was not dull at Burnden Park.

In parallels with modern-day football, where visiting sides to Old Trafford set out with only one man up front, Bolton, defying the traditions of the day, adopted a defensive approach by playing 'only' three up front. The change had the desired effect of preventing a rout and Bolton were never out of contention as a result.

In fact, the opening goal was possibly against the run of play, Jimmy Turnbull breasting down the ball halfway between the circle and the penalty area before beating Jack Stanley and the Bolton centre-forward Albert Shepherd, back helping out in defence, then advancing to beat John Edmondson from six yards out.

Bolton equalised when Holden, trying desperately to clear a David Stokes cross, only succeeded in presenting the ball to John Boyd, whose fierce drive made it 1–1 on 33 minutes.

The winning goal was a classic, Burgess blocking a Bolton attack to feed Bannister, whose ball inside released James Turnbull, whose mazy 40-yard run helped create the space for a wonderful curling goal.

The result left Ernest Mangnall's side five points clear of The Wednesday, who had crashed to a heavy defeat by three goals to nil at Liverpool, and Bury, who had drawn 0–0 at home to Notts County.

Top of the table

Team	Played	Points
Man Utd	10	18
The Wednesday	10	13
Bury	12	13
Man City	9	12

Lancashire Senior Cup

Date: Monday 28 October 1907

Result: Oldham Athletic 3, Manchester United 1

Venue: Hyde Road

Attendance: 8,000

Two goals from Frank Hesham and a single effort from Alex Whaites were enough for Second Division Oldham to beat the runaway Division One leaders, for whom Sandy Turnbull had equalised just before half-time. Oldham went on to beat Preston in the Final to win the competition for the first time.

Frank Hesham was later killed on active service with the Royal Garrison Artillery Regiment in France in 1915.

League Match 11

Against: Birmingham (Away)

Date: Saturday 2 November 1907

Attendance: 20,000

Result: Birmingham 3, Manchester United 4

Birmingham ✪ ✪ ✪

Team: Robinson, Glover, Stokes, Beer, Wigmore, Cornan, Peplow, Green, Jones, Tickle, Eyre.

Scorers: Jones, Eyre (2)

Manchester United ✪ ✪ ✪ ✪

Team: Moger, Holden, Burgess, Duckworth, Roberts, Bell, Meredith, Bannister, J. Turnbull, Picken, Wall.

Scorers: J. Turnbull, Meredith (2), Wall

With Birmingham struggling at the bottom of the League the news that William Henry 'Billy' Jones was fit enough to play after a lengthy absence due to injury was a big boost to the West Midlands side. He was a popular player with the Birmingham fans and earned the nickname of the 'Tipton Smasher' for scoring over 100 goals in just over 250 appearances between 1908–09 and 1912–13.

With the home half-backs finding it difficult to keep pace with the United forwards it was no great surprise when the League leaders struck on 15 minutes, James Turnbull gathering a centre and driving the ball home. Any thoughts that this might lead to another United rout was quickly dispelled when almost from the kick-off Billy Peplow crossed for Jones to head the equaliser. Five minutes later United were back in the lead when Meredith nipped between Frank Cornan and Frank Stokes and from a narrow angle beat Nat Robinson with a powerful drive. Birmingham were level within two minutes, Ninty Eyre heading home, and at half-time the score remained 2–2.

Having played so superbly in the second half at both Newcastle and Blackburn could Mangnall's men do so again? The answer was yes, and in the 55th minute Meredith again broke through the home defence to leave Nat Robinson with no chance to make it 3–2. Two minutes later Duckworth passed to Wall, who from 12 yards out made it 4–2. In the 89th minute Birmingham, who had never stopped trying, reduced the arrears when Eyre scored his second goal.

Despite the fact that seven goals were scored *The Athletic News* was full of praise for both 'keepers, who they felt had both performed admirably. Bell was rated the best back on the field and Meredith was seen as the best player overall, although Jones was also lavishly praised. It had been another fine game and both teams were cheered as they left the pitch.

League Match 12

Against: Everton (Home)

Date: Saturday 9 November 1907

Attendance: 30,000

Result: Manchester United 4, Everton 3

Referee: T. Robertson of Glasgow.

Manchester United ✪✪✪✪

Team: Moger, Holden, Burgess, Duckworth, Roberts, Bell, Meredith, Bannister, J. Turnbull, A. Turnbull, Wall.

Scorers: Meredith, Roberts, Wall (2)

Everton ✪✪✪

Team: Scott, W. Balmer, R. Balmer, Makepeace, Taylor, Abbott, Sharp, Bolton, Young, Settle, H.P. Hardman.

Scorers: Bolton, Hardman, Settle

This was one of the best games ever played at Bank Street, and although United were the eventual winners the match could have gone either way.

Everton, Cup finalists in the two previous seasons with success in 1905–06, were a fine side and on a soft slippery surface they were first into their stride, Alex Young and Jimmy Settle both firing shots narrowly wide. The Merseyside team were also not without aggression and their rough tactics were eventually to lead to captain Walter Balmer being spoken to by the referee in the first half. The Everton right-back was, however, unable to do anything when Meredith slipped past him to give Billy Scott no chance for the game's opening goal. As had happened at Birmingham the previous week United conceded an equaliser within 60 seconds. It came when Hugh Bolton and Settle broke through leaving the former to score on 30 minutes. At half-time the score was 1–1 and there was relief for the home crowd when Wall returned to the field after missing the last 12 minutes of the first period due to injury.

Roberts gave United the lead when he headed home a Meredith corner, and the Welshman then twice broke beyond the Everton backs to pull the ball back for Wall to crash home the third and fourth goals. Everton, 4–1 down, were stung, and they piled forward, and with five minutes left Harold Hardman, with a good shot, made it 4–2. Two minutes later Moger dropped the ball and it was poked home by Settle.

With United pushed back there was panic in the defence and Moger atoned for his earlier mistake when he dived bravely to prevent Harry Makepeace equalising. When the referee blew the whistle for the end of the game there were huge cheers around the ground. The home side had won, but only because they accepted the three opportunities made by Meredith during a five-minute spell at the start of the second half. On another day the result might well have been reversed, especially as both Everton wing-men, Jack Sharp and the amateur Harold P. Hardman, were a constant threat with Holden, in particular, enjoying a difficult afternoon at right-back for United.

Meredith praised

Everton were rated by *The Athletic News* as the best team seen so far at Clayton and would have undoubtedly gained at least a point if it had not been for Meredith, about whom *The Athletic News* voiced the opinion that 'no forward in the country has played better this season'. High praise indeed, but that was nothing compared to *The Manchester Courier* who reported that 'Meredith emphasises each week that he is the greatest player of this or any age, not only scoring but having a part in all three other goals.' The paper turned to Shakespeare in their praise of the Welsh winger, saying: 'Age does not wither him nor custom stake his infinite variety' – and current United fans reckon Giggs is a good player!

Harry Makepeace

Harry Makepeace is unique in the world of sport as he is the only man to win an FA Cup and League Championship-winners' medal (both with Everton), be capped as a soccer international (with England four times), win a County Cricket Championship medal (with Lancashire on four occasions) and be capped as a cricket international (four England caps versus Australia in 1920–21). What odds would you get with the bookmakers for anyone doing that nowadays?

League Match 13

Against: Sunderland (Away)

Date: Saturday 16 November 1907

Attendance: 30,000

Result: Sunderland 1, Manchester United 2

Referee: F. Heath of Birmingham.

Sunderland

Team: Ward, Bonthron, Daykin, Tait, Jarvie, Low, Raine, Hogg, Raybould, Holley, Bridgett.

Scorer: Raybould

Manchester United ⚽ ⚽

Team: Moger, Holden, Burgess, Duckworth, Roberts, Bell, Meredith, Bannister, A. Turnbull, Picken, Wall.

Scorers: A. Turnbull, own-goal

With eight consecutive League victories the question was 'Who will stop Manchester United?' The next to try were Sunderland, who with four League titles to their name were only one behind record holders Aston Villa. The Wearsiders were in 13th place in the table, but they had only been beaten once at home in six games, a 5–2 opening–day reverse against Manchester City. The Sunderland side contained the former United man Bonthron. The report that follows is taken from *The Newcastle Journal*:

Sunderland made a brilliant attempt to halt the all-conquering march of Manchester United at Roker Park and were rather unfortunate to be beaten by the odd goal in three. The goal came from Bonthron when the greasy ball accidentally spooned off his toe and into the net. Bonthron had played a powerful game against his old club, and Daykin and the half-backs also acquitted themselves nobly in checking the speedy and masterly moves of the United front rank.

Indeed, they did their work so well that neither Meredith nor Wall made any impression in the game, unlike when they played at Newcastle. The aggression of the home forwards was a revelation and they were individually cleverer than United throughout the first half, with Raine and Hogg the principal performers in a thrilling struggle. Their shooting, too, was accurate and deadly but Moger could not be beaten. United certainly played a superb all-round game but the men who were instrumental in repelling Sunderland's sterling attacks were Moger and Roberts.

Roberts in particular was a giant in strength and resource. James Turnbull kicked-off for United and a well-timed pass from Jarvie was collected by Hogg in the first minute and he evaded the defenders with all his old time dash and skill. Despite being wide of the goal he sent in an accurate drive but saw the ball strike the top of the upright in what was a narrow escape for the visitors. For fully five minutes the Sunderland forwards displayed a wonderful command of the ball and Bridgett twice threatened Moger's goal.

Raybould wasted a rare opportunity by needlessly handling the ball as high tension and earnestness manifested itself in Sunderland's play. Indeed, the football was of a high quality and perhaps even excelled that played in the days of the 'Team of all Talents' who were so ably led by the late Johnny Campbell. Wall and A. Turnbull broke away with a fast dribble but they were neatly intercepted by Tait, who twice put his forwards in a good position. Holden and Burgess, however, were invincible and kicked a great length.

Hogg and Bridgett lobbed the ball into the goalmouth and the ball was only partially cleared to Low who sent in a terrific 30-yard drive but it was charged down. Raybould then went very close with a capital drive. For the first 15 minutes the balance of play was unquestionably in Sunderland's favour, and when Hogg raced through on to a pass from Raybould a goal was keenly anticipated.

His shot was good but Moger made a good save. A few minutes later Hogg was within inches of getting past Burgess and Bridgett too was conspicuous for a great effort.

Sunderland were playing with a spirit worthy of their best days and delighted the crowd with their fast, incisive raids. Hogg and Raine worked neatly together and Raine volleyed in a shot that went at a tremendous pace and looked like beating Moger until the custodian leapt to deflect the ball past the post. At last United crossed the halfway line and Bannister had an opening but shot weakly into Ward's hands. This was quickly followed by a promising move between Hogg and Raine with the latter sending in a shot that almost squeezed into the net.

Wall luckily forced a corner off Bonthron and from the nicely placed flag-kick Roberts got in a straight drive that Jarvie blocked. United forced another corner shortly afterwards and A. Turnbull was just beaten to the ball by Ward. Sunderland had taken all the honours so far both individually and collectively as United were compelled to defend to combat the severe pressure from the home side. Sunderland again illuminated a magnificent exhibition with a spirited effort initiated by Low, who passed the ball to Bridgett. He swung it into the middle, where the unmarked Hogg sent in a brilliant but abortive effort flying barely an inch too high with Moger beaten all the way. Thereafter Meredith stood out for the first time with his great pace but he was charged off the ball by Jarvie at the critical moment. Around now Meredith revealed his best form and with his sweeping stride forced another fruitless corner. As the interval approached a feature of the United defence was the superb form of Roberts who artfully checked the home forwards.

On one occasion, however, Raybould and his teammates completely tied up the United full-backs and Moger was legitimately charged when holding the ball by Raybould, Hogg and Holley in turn. The referee, however, was at fault when he penalised the home side. Rain began falling after half-time and for a few moments United greatly threatened the Sunderland goal with a score almost coming from a corner-kick. Barely five minutes into the second half Bridgett got through with a pretty effort but he finished weakly.

Sunderland came again with an irresistible dash and forced a corner on the right. The kick was poorly placed by Raine but a United half-back* headed the ball back towards his own goal and Raybould pounced to neatly head through. The goal provoked tremendous enthusiasm but within a couple of minutes Meredith surprised Low almost on the goalline and squared the ball for A. Turnbull to equalise with a header. There was now greater variety and pace in United's moves and when A. Turnbull centred Bonthron unluckily pushed the ball into his own goal.

Undaunted Sunderland immediately stormed back with magnificent efforts. United continued to attack and after an exciting mêlée in front of goal Turnbull volleyed the ball hard against the bar from 18 yards. After about 25 minutes of the second half there was a marked revival in Sunderland play and Raine and

Hogg forced a couple of corners. The second of these was well placed by Raine and Moger was lucky to gather a sharp header from Raybould.

The visiting full-backs and Moger successfully resisted a supreme effort by the Roker forwards in the last five minutes and Sunderland left the field beaten rather unluckily. The official return showed that 30,852 people passed through the turnstiles with receipts being no less than £1,050-4s-3d. A tenth of this, or £105-12s, has been given to the town's distress fund.

(*Newcastle Journal*)

*The ball was, in fact, headed back by James Turnbull – as reported in *The Athletic News*.

League Match 14

Against: Arsenal (Home) – United complete first 10-match winning run in their history.

Date: Saturday 23 November 1907

Attendance: 10,000

Result: Manchester United 4, Woolwich Arsenal 2

Referee: F.H. Dennis of Middlesbrough.

Manchester United

✪ ✪ ✪ ✪

Team: Moger, Holden, Burgess, Duckworth, Roberts, Bell, Meredith, Bannister, J. Turnbull, A. Turnbull, Williams.

Scorer: A. Turnbull (4)

Arsenal ⚽ ⚽

Team: Ashcroft, Gray, Sharp, Dick, Sands, McEachrane, Garbutt, Coleman, Kyle, C. Satterthwaite, Neave.

Scorers: Garbutt, Kyle

The teams provided marvellous entertainment in this game for a rain-soaked crowd of 10,000 on a wet pitch, that long before the end was little more than a mud bath, particularly down the middle of the field. *The Athletic News*: 'I suppose most grounds were bad at the weekend, but for a picture of unloveliness I fancy Clayton would be hard to beat.'

Arsenal arrived in Manchester with 13 points from 13 games and in ninth place in the table. They were behind within two minutes, when Jimmy Ashcroft was beaten by Sandy Turnbull's low drive, but the 'keeper then kept his side in the game with a fine save from a Roberts shot. Arsenal threatened Moger's goal but David Neave shot over the bar with only the 'keeper to beat, before Bannister hit the bar with a shot from 15 yards. On 32 minutes the League leaders made it 2–0 when after James Turnbull missed Billy Meredith's cross his colleague Sandy Turnbull was on hand to prod the ball home. Arsenal were lucky shortly afterwards when another Roberts shot beat Ashcroft but came back into play off the bar. The Gunners showed they still had some fight in them when just before half-time they fashioned, but missed, two chances when both Peter Kyle and Neave might have done better.

On 55 minutes the away side were back in the game when William Garbutt tricked Burgess and from 20 yards beat Moger, who, like Ashcroft in the opposite goal, was ankle-deep in mud. Two minutes later the United 'keeper dropped a Neave high ball and Kyle was on hand to touch it home to make it 2–2. Were Manchester United going to drop their first point since way back in August?

The answer was no, although there was disappointment for Harry Williams, who, playing as a replacement for Wall, out injured with a bruised thigh, missed two good chances.

United retook the lead from a great Sandy Turnbull header following a curling cross into the box from Duckworth after the Arsenal defence had scrambled Meredith's corner away. The goal brought scenes of great rejoicing among the home crowd, and they were even happier when, following an Archie Gray miskick, Williams pulled the ball back for Sandy Turnbull to score his fourth goal to make it 4–2.

Afterwards the newspaper reports praised both sides for producing such a fine display, and although Sandy Turnbull was clearly the Man of the Match with four goals there was again great praise for the United half-back line up, with 'Mancunian' in *Sport and Field* stating: 'It was where the game was won.' Although Williams had done his best all agreed that he was never going to replace Wall in the side, and without ever playing in the first XI again he moved on to Leeds City in the following summer after playing 36 times for United and scoring eight goals.

League Match 15

Against: The Wednesday (Away)
Date: Saturday 30 November 1907
Attendance: 40,000
Result: The Wednesday 2, Manchester United 0
Referee: J.H. Pearson of Crewe.

The Wednesday   ⚽ ⚽

Team: Lyall, Layton, Burton, Brittleton, Crawshaw, Bartlett, Chapman, Bradshaw, Wilson, Stewart, Simpson.

Scorers: Bartlett, Stewart

Manchester United

Team: Moger, Holden, Burgess, Duckworth, Roberts, Bell, Meredith, Bannister, J. Turnbull, A. Turnbull, Wall.

Victory for the home side before their then record attendance brought to an end Manchester United's magnificent winning streak of 10 consecutive League victories that had commenced on 21 September when Sheffield United had been beaten 2–1 at Bank Street.

The Wednesday – 'Sheffield' was only incorporated into their name in 1929 – had won the First Division title in 1902–03 and 1903–04 and now there were hopes of a third success. They were lying second and a win would cut United's lead to four points.

For the first time in the season the home side were able to call upon the exact XI that had played so superbly to beat Everton 2–1 in the previous season's FA Cup Final, a result that saw Wednesday capture the trophy for the second time.

The match proved worthy of such a fine crowd, and few, including a great many from Manchester, who saw it must have left disappointed by the entertainment on offer. United were the better side in the first half, with Meredith constantly threatening to get beyond the home defence. On more than one occasion Jack Lyall in the home goal produced a superb save, with both Turnbulls, Wall and Meredith all denied at various points during the first 45 minutes.

Just before half-time, however, Frank Bradshaw, the Wednesday inside-right, seemed certain to send his side into the lead but he froze, when after beating the United defence he fired well wide with only Moger to beat. Bradshaw was to win his only England cap at the end of the season, scoring a hat-trick in an 11–1 victory in Austria, thus becoming the fifth and, to date, last player to score three goals on their only international appearance for England.

Things looked bleak for the home side when it became clear that the side's playmaker at centre-half, Tom Crawshaw, was only fit enough to limp out the match on the far right, forcing a reshuffle that saw little Harry Chapman move back from his outside-right position to play centre-half. Chapman, whose brother Herbert is arguably English football's greatest ever manager with First Division and FA Cup success at Huddersfield Town in the 1920s and Arsenal in the 1930s, was to show great versatility. With Billy Bartlett finally getting to grips with Meredith, United were for once proving second best as the crowd roared on Wednesday. And it was Bartlett who opened the scoring with a shot that left Harry Moger helpless.

The away side thought they should have had a penalty shortly afterwards but the referee decided, to the disappointment of the United players, that Harry Burton had not handled. The disappointment increased when Burgess was ruled to have handled a George Simpson effort, but Moger kept his side in the contest with a fine save from the resulting penalty from Tom Brittleton. However, the United 'keeper was subsequently given no chance when Andrew Wilson, for once escaping Roberts's attention, forced an opening for Jimmy Stewart, scorer of the opening goal at the 1907 FA Cup Final, to drive his side into an unassailable lead. It might have been three shortly afterwards but Chapman's shot hit the bar rather than entering the goal.

The result reduced United's lead at the top of the table to four points. Not that the side had played badly, with *The Sheffield Independent*'s reporter at the match commenting afterwards: 'A very fine all round side are Manchester Utd; and despite their failure to get through Saturday's great ordeal successfully, they will probably win the League Championship all the same.'

In a fine home performance Lyall, Chapman and Bartlett were selected as the best of the bunch by the *Sheffield Independent* match reporter.

Top of the table

Team	Played	Points
Man Utd	15	26
The Wednesday	15	22
Newcastle Utd	15	17
Man City	15	17

Andrew Wilson

Scotsman Wilson had moved to Sheffield in 1900 from Clyde and was to play for The Wednesday until March 1920, during which time he appeared for the team on 545 occasions and scored 216 goals, records which still stand. He was capped six times for his country.

Players' Union, 2 December 1907

Manchester United's remarkable run to the top of Division One did not necessarily mean the players were happy with their lot. Like many other professional footballers they were angered by the maximum wage limit that restricted pay to just £4 a week even though gates were booming.

They were also rightly concerned about the way clubs treated their players and could recall that when Jimmy Ross, the Preston North End, Liverpool and Manchester City legendary scorer, had been forced to retire early on ill-health grounds (which ultimately led to his death at just 36 in 1902) he had been unable to save any money for his wife and children.

Then, in April 1907, Thomas Blackstock, a Manchester United reserve full-back with 38 first-team appearances since his move to the club from Cowdenbeath in June 1903, died during a Lancashire Combination fixture against St Helens Recs. At the subsequent inquest a verdict of 'natural causes' was returned and his family received no compensation, a fate also experienced by the family of Manchester City's left-back David Jones who died during a pre-season game in 1902, leaving the club to claim he had not been 'working' at the time.

In February 1898 Ross had joined with other top players, including Preston's Bob Holmes, John Devey of Aston Villa and John Cameron of Everton, to form a trade union that they called the Association Footballers' Union (AFU). Central to their demands was for negotiations regarding transfers to be between the interested club and the player concerned rather than, as was the case at the time, between the clubs with the player excluded. The players' struggle was badly wounded when several players were lured by the higher wages then on offer in the Southern League, with Cameron, for example, joining Tottenham Hotspur. Negotiations with the Football League thus ended in failure and in May 1900 the Football Association's AGM agreed to set a maximum wage of professional footballers in the Football League at just £4 a week.

It was against this background that several of the players at Manchester United, including Charlie Roberts, Herbert Burgess, Sandy Turnbull, Charlie Sagar and Billy Meredith, set out to form a new Players' Union. The first meeting was held on 2 December 1907 at the Imperial Hotel, Manchester. Meredith chaired the meeting that was attended by around 500 professional footballers, and the Association Football Players' Union (AFPU) was formed.

Although most clubs were happy to maintain the £4 ceiling on wages the larger ones would have been happy to have seen it scrapped as they could have then lured the better players to play for them. As Manchester United were now one of these clubs it was hardy surprising that, initially at least, both the club's owner John Henry Davies and president John J. Bentley backed the players' campaign. Both were to subsequently change their attitudes when negotiations between the AFPU and the FA broke down the following season, following which the FA ordered all players to leave the Union by 1 July 1909. Most players duly did as they were told, but not so those of Manchester United and 17 players from Sunderland.

All of the United side were suspended by the club but to their credit remained steadfast in their beliefs, and it was not until 31 August 1909 that the FA agreed to allow the players to remain in what was a Union clearly weakened by the actions of the players from other sides who had not stuck to their principles. When the team subsequently turned out in the first match of the 1909–10 season the following day all the players wore AFPU armbands. Meredith, knowing that the maximum wage and the retain and transfer system was to remain in place, said it was clear that footballers as a whole had lost the struggle. He commented: 'The unfortunate thing is that so many players refuse to take things seriously but are content to live a kind of schoolboy life and to do just what they are told...instead of thinking and acting for himself and his class.' It was to be many, many years before footballers were to get the rewards their skills deserved, and although those United players who led the way in the early 20th century were allowed to continue playing, some did suffer for their principles, with Charlie Roberts subsequently missing out on a benefit game that was worth approximately £500 to him, more than two years' wages at the time. Others suffered in less obvious ways by being overlooked for England when selectors came to pick the side, and this undoubtedly accounts for why Roberts only played three times for his country.

League Match 16

Against: Bristol City (Home)

Date: Saturday 7 December 1907

Attendance: 20,000

Result: Manchester United 2, Bristol City 1

Manchester United

Team: Moger, Holden, Stacey, Duckworth, Roberts, Bell, Meredith, Bannister, J. Turnbull, A. Turnbull, Wall.

Scorer: Wall (2)

Bristol City

Team: Lewis, Annan, Cottle, Spear, Wedlock, Hanlin, Staniforth, Maxwell, Gilligan, Burton, Hilton.

Scorer: Hilton

Having lost their first match in 11 games the League leaders had a chance to get back to winning ways with a home game against the side that had beaten United to top spot in Division Two during their 1905–06 promotion season. By doing so City had become the first side outside the Midlands and North to capture either the First and Second Division titles (Arsenal were the first Southern side to win Division One in 1930–31).

Bristol City arrived in Manchester on the back of an easy home victory against Nottingham Forest by three goals to nil, a result that had taken The Robins up to fourth place in the table but nine points behind the leaders.

Despite the defeat in Sheffield, there was only one change in the United line up, Stacey being re-introduced because Burgess had broken down in training. It was a sparse crowd when the teams ran out to play on a pitch almost totally devoid of grass which was certain to become a mud bath after persistent rain overnight.

Late spectators would have missed the captains needing three attempts to decide the toss after the coin of the referee, Mr J. Mason of Burslem, twice became stuck in the mud. It was not the most auspicious of starts, especially as just prior to kick-off a strong wind had also decided to make an appearance, which Bristol City were asked to kick into after Roberts eventually won the toss.

It took United less than a minute to show their talents, Meredith hitting a fierce drive that the City 'keeper George Lewis did well to hold. The Bristol man then had to fling himself across the goal to block a Sandy Turnbull effort. A James Turnbull header then seemed set to open the scoring only for the ball to hit his colleague Bannister. It seemed it was only a matter of time before a goal was scored and on seven minutes that was just what happened when Bristol City, who had hardly been out of their own half never mind forced Moger into a decent save, took the lead to shock a crowd that had risen above 20,000.

Following an attack down the Bristol right a Stacey clearance was blocked, and when the ball seemed destined to end up in the net Holden's desperate efforts to clear simply ended up presenting a grateful Frank Hilton with an open goal. From the restart the home side were back on the attack, but their confidence had clearly been shaken as few scoring opportunities were created. The away side might even have increased their lead when Hilton was clean through, but just as he went to shoot Duckworth dived in bravely to clear the ball to safety.

Meredith then brought the home crowd alive by a scintillating dribbling run before pulling the ball back for Wall, whose shot was heading for the net before Archie Annan acrobatically kicked the ball away. The outside-left was not to be denied for long, however, and as City pushed up the field he used his pace in a driving run that ended with him flashing the ball past Lewis before he crashed into the post and had to be afterwards revived by the United trainer Fred Bacon. On his return he was given a tremendous ovation from the crowd and showed he was far from finished by then hitting another shot just wide. Lewis then kept the scores with a great save from Jimmy Turnbull, and at half-time it was still 1–1.

It should have been 2–1 to United within seconds of the restart but Meredith, for once, was guilty of a wild attempt on goal from just a dozen yards out. In the circumstances it might therefore have been better to have allowed someone else to take the penalty that the home side won courtesy of another sparkling Wall run shortly afterwards. Meredith, however, was given the task and fired well wide.

Wall, who at half-time had been presented with a magnificent bronze statue from a Mr G.E. Howarth in recognition of having taken part in 50 successive League games, was not to be put off. However, when he pulled back the ball from the byline his forward colleagues could not make up their minds as to who should have a shot and the chance was wasted.

With the pitch by now almost unplayable the game became one long hard slog, and with both sides noticeably tiring another goal seemed unlikely.

The magnificent Wall had other ideas, dribbling the ball across the box before hitting a fine 80th-minute shot that the Bristol 'keeper could only watch whistle by into the net.

With the rain pouring down Bristol pushed forward in search of an equaliser, and with the players all virtually covered from head to toe in mud it was almost impossible for the spectators to be sure who was who. They could, however, watch the side from the South West mount wave after wave of attack, and Roberts was forced to desperately hack the ball to safety before a fine, last-second diving save from Moger helped ensure two valuable points. With Blackburn beating The Wednesday, it restored Manchester United's lead at the top of Division One to six points. Considering the conditions, it had been a remarkably good game with Wall outstanding and fully deserving his two goals.

League Match 17

Against: Notts County (Away)

Date: Saturday 14 December 1907

Attendance: 11,000

Result: Notts County 1, Manchester United 1

Notts County

Team: Iremonger, Morley, Montgomery, Emberton, Clamp, Craythorne, Dean, Matthews, Tarplin, F. Jones, Munroe.

Scorer: Jones

Manchester United

Team: Moger, Holden, Burgess, Duckworth, Roberts, Bell, Meredith, Bannister, J. Turnbull, A. Turnbull, Wall.

Scorer: Meredith

Formed in 1862, Notts County are the oldest professional League club in the world, and when United travelled to play them in December 1907 they faced a club who were among the original 12 Football League members in 1888. County then played their home games at Trent Bridge county cricket ground, not moving to their current ground Meadow Lane until September 1910. Although they had never won the League title they had captured the FA Cup in 1894. In the Final, in which they beat Bolton Wanderers 4–1 at Goodison Park, Jimmy Logan became the second player to score an FA Cup Final hat-trick, following Blackburn Rover's Billy Townley into the record books.

County had beaten United 3–0 at home in January 1907 during the previous season, so the result would be another indication of just how far Ernest Mangnall's side had travelled in a year. County entered the match in 12th place with 15 points from 17 games, but had suffered a disappointment the previous weekend when they were beaten 2–0 by near neighbours Forest.

In goal for County was Albert Iremonger. He was well known for his outspoken nature on the football pitch, which was to lead to the end of his 222 consecutive appearances. Iremonger would often leave his goalmouth to contest decisions made by match officials, sometimes ending up in the centre of the pitch. He still holds the record for the most appearances for County at 601, of which 37 were in the FA Cup. Iremonger also played county cricket for Nottinghamshire from 1906 to 1910.

As was the custom, County, on winning the toss elected to play with the wind, but despite this it was the away side who played the better in the first 45 minutes. Their captain, Roberts, led them magnificently, ignoring the elements to pass the ball out to the wings for Meredith and Wall to attack Jock Montgomery and Herbert Morley respectively. It also meant that the ball avoided getting bogged down in the mud which clogged up the middle of the field.

It was Meredith who gave Manchester United the lead with five minutes of the first half remaining, when collecting a Roberts pass he screwed the ball with his left foot across the goal and into the net for a great goal. With United leading 1–0 at half-time and now playing with the wind another win was very much on the cards, and it appeared certain when Meredith's shot appeared to be grabbed from behind the line by Iremonger on 55 minutes; however, the referee was unable to say for certain that it had crossed the line and County survived. Two minutes later the home side equalised when Walter Tarplin created an opening for Fred Jones to beat Moger. This was to mark the start of County's best spell of the game, with Jerry Dean giving Burgess and Bell down the United left a torrid time as County searched for the winner.

The final score of 1–1 represented an advance of a point on the previous season's result at Trent Bridge, and meant that, while The Wednesday had won, United's lead at the top, as the halfway point in the League loomed, was a healthy five points. It all meant that the United players were in fine heart as they departed on the Monday after the game for two weeks' special training at Norbreck; although they also had a derby match with Manchester City to look forward to the following weekend.

League Match 18

Against: Man City (Home)

Date: Saturday 21 December 1907

Attendance: 35,000

Result: Manchester United 3, Manchester City 1

Referee: T. Campbell.

Manchester United   ✪ ✪ ✪

Team: Moger, Holden, Burgess, Duckworth, Roberts, Bell, Meredith, Bannister, J. Turnbull, A. Turnbull, Wall.

Scorers: Wall, A. Turnbull (2)

Sent off: A. Turnbull

Manchester City

Team: Smith, Hill, Norgrove, Buchan, Eadie, Blair, Dorsett, Wood, Thornley, Jones, Conlin.

Scorer: Eadie

Having beaten Manchester City twice already in the Lancashire and Manchester Senior Cups, United must have entered the arena in confident form. Although City were sixth in the League they were a long way behind the League leaders with 11 fewer points, although they did have a game in hand. City had beaten Nottingham Forest the previous weekend 4–2.

Despite it being only days before Christmas, when money was no doubt tight, the game's attraction saw the then largest ever crowd of 35,000 assemble at Bank Street, and both teams received the cheers of their supporters when they ran on to the pitch.

Despite the already intense rivalry between the two clubs, previous games between them had been relatively free of ill feeling. There was to be little indication of the 'season of goodwill' on show on this occasion, however, during which Sandy Turnbull became the first player to be sent off in a Manchester derby. Afterwards there was considerable criticism of George Dorsett for falling over so theatrically when it appeared that he had received only the slightest of flicks from the United man's outstretched arm on his neck in the 55th minute. The City man later told reporters the blow had chopped off his wind, which was reported in *The Manchester Courier* as at least 'explaining what appeared to be a silly attempt on the part of the City player to make the assault look a bad one.' Not everyone at the match might have agreed, but the incident had the effect of turning an already rough game into a brawl for the next 10 minutes before both sets of players saw sense and settled back down to play football.

The state of the pitch was poor at the start and got worse as the game progressed, with the final stages being played on a mud bath. United showed themselves to be a far superior side, adapting to the conditions almost from the off and employing their wingmen throughout to great effect. Meredith appeared to have been singled out for special attention, as according to *The Manchester Courier* match report he 'got more hard knocks than he has received for some time.' The ex-City man was to have the final laugh, however, playing a part in two of the home side's three goals.

The League leaders had gone ahead through Wall who, following up a fine double save by Walter Smith from Meredith and Sandy Turnbull, found the net with a shot that must have hurt the 'keeper as it entered the net off the side of his face.

Despite pushing forward, only once after that did City seem likely to fashion an equaliser when John Wood was guilty of a bad miss after Jimmy Conlin's ball had split the United rearguard. It was therefore no great surprise when Sandy Turnbull headed home a Meredith free-kick to make it 2–0. With half-time approaching Billy 'Lot' Jones and Conlin missed decent opportunities to send their team in just a goal down.

The match as a contest was over within minutes of the second half getting underway, when Frank Norgrove was dispossessed by Sandy Turnbull, who scored his second goal of the game to make it 3–0. City were down but they then managed to pull a goal back when Bill Eadie headed home from a corner. When, just 10 minutes after Turnbull's dismissal, Burgess limped off with an injury likely to keep him out of the side for the next few matches, the way was open for City to grab a point.

It was at this point that the United defence of Moger, Holden, Roberts, Bell and Duckworth dug deep, playing the final 24 minutes of the game as though their very existence depended on winning the match. When the referee blew the final whistle, United had won a famous victory.

In the light of the sending off of Sandy Turnbull and the unpleasant incidents that followed, the referee Mr F.J. Wall's match report to the FA was later released to the newspapers. He said:

'In the first half I had occasion to warn and then caution Turnbull upon his conduct, and in the second half he struck Dorsett of Manchester City in the face with the back of his hand. I at once ordered him off.

'The blow was certainly a mild one and undoubtedly Turnbull received provocation from the attitude Dorsett took up, but in the face of the previous caution I had no option.

'I regret that for some little time after the players on both sides appeared to lose their heads and indulged in childish and irresponsible tactics that, to say the least of it, were anything but creditable to them and yet not of sufficient character to enable me to carry out the greater powers invested in me.' P.J. Wall, Esq, F.A. 22 December 1907.

Meanwhile, in the match's aftermath the newspapers saw fit to run a series of cartoon drawings on events at Bank Street, with *The Manchester Courier* showing a retreating bedraggled City army, two sets of players engaging in arm-to-arm combat in the middle of the field and finally one of Dorsett falling theatrically with the referee rushing to send Turnbull from the field. Turnbull would now have to go before the FA committee, who would decide whether to suspend him.

League Match 19

Against: Bury (Home)

Date: Wednesday 25 December 1907

Attendance: 45,000

Result: Manchester United 2, Bury 1

Manchester United ⚽ ⚽

Team: Moger, Holden, Stacey, Duckworth, Roberts, Bell, Meredith, Bannister, J. Turnbull, A. Turnbull, Wall.

Scorers: J. Turnbull, Meredith

Bury ⚽

Team: Raeside, Lindsey, McMahon, Dewhurst, Davidson, Roe, Gildea, Currie, Hibbert, Kay, Booth.

Scorer: Currie

An even larger crowd than the one that assembled for the City game were present to see United take on near neighbours and title rivals Bury on Christmas Day in 1907. Today, of course, there would be no prospect of sides playing on 25 December, but it was, in fact, only at the end of the 1956–57 season that a full Football League programme on Christmas Day was ended. Some clubs continued to play on and it was not until 1965 that Blackpool and Blackburn played the last-ever Christmas Day fixture in England, with Blackpool winning 4–2.

If any of the Bury or United players were upset at having to play on Christmas Day then what of the Bristol City side, who on 25 December 1907 played an away game at Sunderland, the team having left Bristol the previous week to play Bolton Wanderers on the 21st and returned after another away game on Boxing Day at Everton before playing at home to Birmingham City on 28 December. Amazingly, Bristol won one and drew three of the four games.

In 1907–08 Archibald Montgomery, an ex-United goalkeeper who had made just three appearances for the club in September 1905, all of which were won, managed Bury. Unable to shift Harry Moger as number one he had returned to Bury and been appointed manager in February 1907. Unlike their near neighbours, Bury had previously captured a major trophy by winning the FA Cup in 1900 and 1903, beating Derby County 6–0 in the second match to record what remains the largest Cup Final victory.

According to *The Manchester Courier* those present saw 'a game that was one of the best possible to witness, not only for the excellence of the play, but also for the uncertainty which attended it. No one could wish to see better, and it was rendered all the more attractive through the attacks to which first one goal and then the other was subjected.'

With Burgess's thigh not having recovered from an injury sustained during the City game four days previously there was a recall for Stacey at left-back. Bury decided to replace Joe Leeming at full-back with Johnny McMahon, who Montgomery felt was better placed to combat Meredith. It did not prove to be the case.

It was the away side that showed first, when Billy Hibbert was put clean through but, failing to steady himself, he crashed his shot well wide. Roberts then showed real quality by dribbling the ball out of defence to set up a series of attacks down both wings, leading to the great crowd cheering his every move. Jimmy Lindsey, the Bury half-back, was fortunate to see a shot from Sandy Turnbull cannon off him and miss the post by inches. This marked the start of some fierce home pressure, and in the 16th minute it was no surprise when they took the lead. Wall had been surprisingly quiet but his cross was so good that all James Turnbull had to do was touch it home. Tom Kay should have made it 1–1 within seconds but, like Hibbert earlier, he failed even to force Moger to save.

The United goalkeeper showed just how good he was seconds afterwards, diving full length to turn away Tom Booth's shot for a corner.

As half-time of an end-to-end game approached Wall somehow conspired to put the ball wide from just yards out. The United left-winger soon came again, squaring a lovely ball to Meredith who, taking the ball in his stride, hit the ball back across the goal and into the net off the post with James Raeside well beaten. This meant that at half-time United led 2–0.

Bury were determined to get themselves back into the game once it restarted and they pressed the home XI back towards their own goal. Billy Gildea seemed to be everywhere, dashing down one wing and then the other, shooting on sight and inspiring his colleagues. The goal Bury deserved duly arrived, although today it would be disallowed as after Moger caught a dropping cross he was shoulder-charged by Kay, causing him to drop the ball, and after it was pushed into the middle Bob Currie got the final touch to it. This roused Bury to even greater efforts, but standing in their way were Holden and Stacey, who both defended magnificently, the latter playing his finest game so far for Mangnall's side.

Having not been seen as an attacking force, United then forced Raeside to show how fine a 'keeper he was, with one shot from Meredith worth the admission price alone.

The last quarter of an hour saw the home side reduced to some desperate defending to hold on to their lead, and Hibbert was desperately unlucky when twice his shots flashed past Moger and narrowly wide. On the balance of the game a draw might have been the right result. Moger had played brilliantly. In fact, both 'keepers could have been proud of their efforts, and Stacey's display at full-back showed he was ready for regular first-team football. Roberts was the best half-back on the field, particularly as his colleagues Duckworth and Bell found it difficult to contain the Bury forwards.

With the teams due to meet on New Year's Day at Gigg Lane there was the prospect of another fine game to kick-off 1908, a year that seemed increasingly likely to see United capture the Division One title.

League Match 20

Against: Preston (Away)

Date: Saturday 28 December 1907

Attendance: 12,000

Result: Preston North End 0, Manchester United 0

Preston

Team: McBride, Winchester, Rodway, McLean, Stringfellow, Lyon, Becton, Dawson, Smith, Wilson, Sanderson.

Manchester United

Team: Moger, Holden, Stacey, Duckworth, Roberts, Bell, Meredith, Bannister, J. Turnbull, A. Turnbull, Wall.

When these teams had last met, at Deepdale in December 1906, a 2–0 victory for the home side helped ensure that Manchester United remained in the bottom half of the table with no prospect of winning their first League title. One year on, with half the League fixtures already completed, the away side were nine points in front of second-placed Newcastle United and seemingly assured of Championship success. Preston lay in mid-table with 18 points from 19 games. With defeats at Middlesbrough and The Wednesday, Ernest Mangnall's side were not in a position to threaten the record of the PNE side that went through the very first League season undefeated in 1888–89. However, with 56 goals and 33 points they had a real chance to break the highest number of goals and points records of 100 and 51 respectively recorded by Sunderland's 'Team of All Talents' in 1892–93 and Liverpool and Newcastle in the previous two seasons.

The crowd was boosted by a considerable travelling support that cheered Roberts as he led his players on to the field. With Burgess again declared unfit there was another chance for Stacey to make his presence felt. Preston had been forced to make changes, Herbert Danson and Joe Derbyshire having being injured playing on Christmas Day against Blackburn. They made way for John Winchester at the back and Benjamin Sanderson at outside-left. This being Christmas time, the ground was frost-bound and there was a strong wind doing its best to disrupt proceedings.

Having won the toss, Roberts went with the custom of the time by deciding to play with the wind. It was Preston who might have scored first but Charlie Dawson headed Tommy Rodway's cross high over the bar. Meredith then had the crowd gasping when after breaking into the box he delicately back-heeled the ball, but Duckworth was slow to react and Billy Lyon cleared up field. The Welshman then forced a shot through a crowded goal area but it flew narrowly wide.

Meredith and Bannister were linking up well and causing all sorts of problems down the Preston left, but with the wind increasing in strength much of the players' efforts were taken up with simply trying to keep the ball in play rather than fashioning chances.

It was something of a miracle as the half-hour mark approached that Preston did not find themselves a goal down when firstly Meredith's shot passed narrowly across the goal with most of the crowd convinced the ball was bound to enter the net, before the winger's cross was only inches from being turned into the net by the diving Sandy Turnbull. The half thus ended without a goal, but considering the conditions it had not been a bad match.

Sadly the second half, while containing some fine play in the middle of the park, rarely saw either 'keeper tested. Preston might have had some excuse as for much of it they were forced to play with just 10 fit men, Percy Smith, their centre-forward, being injured and unable to run. With plenty of the ball there is little doubt that on another day Manchester United would have consequently gone on to win the game, but both Turnbulls, for once, seemed to be leaden-footed and wasted the chances presented to them by Meredith and Wall.

The game ended with a point for each side and it meant that in 1907 the away side had played a total of 37 League games, winning 27, drawing four and losing six, form which if maintained in 1908 was certain to see the First Division trophy on display at Bank Street at the season's end.

First Division League Table on 28 December 1907

Team	Played	Points
Man Utd	20	34
Newcastle Utd	21	25
The Wednesday	20	24
Bury	21	24
Bristol City	21	23
Everton	20	22
Aston Villa	21	21
Notts County	23	21
Woolwich Arsenal	20	20
Preston North End	21	20
Chelsea	21	19
Liverpool	19	18
Sheffield United	19	17
Bolton Wanderers	19	17
Blackburn Rovers	20	17
Middlesbrough	21	17
Nottingham Forest	20	16
Birmingham	21	16
Sunderland	21	15

Manchester United were nine points clear at the top with 18 matches of the season remaining. Could they capture their first major title in 1908?

League Match 21

Against: Bury (Away)

Date: Wednesday 1 January 1908

Attendance: 29,500 – this was Bury's record crowd at the time.

Result: Bury 0, Manchester United 1

Bury

Team: Raeside, Lindsey, McMahon, Dewhurst, Davidson, Roe, Gildea, Currie, Hibbert, Kay, Booth.

Manchester United

Team: Moger, Holden, Stacey, Duckworth, Roberts, Bell, Meredith, Bannister, J. Turnbull, A. Turnbull, Wall.

Scorer: Wall

Both sides were unchanged from the Christmas Day fixture, Bury manager Archie Montgomery no doubt hoping that with home advantage they could reverse the scoreline and by doing so put pressure on the Division One runaway leaders. As expected, there was large crowd and Gigg Lane was packed to the rafters well before kick-off. If the game was even half as good as the game at Bank Street then no one would be able to complain about the entertainment.

Although the weather was remarkably sunny for the first day of the year it was accompanied by a cold, biting and blustery wind that threatened to spoil the game.

Having won the toss the Bury captain Jack Dewhurst, as was usual for the time, chose to set his opponents to face the wind, and it was the home side who pressed at the start. It did not take too long for the first opportunity when a Stacey clearance lacked distance, but Bob Currie, the Bury inside-right, shot wide. Billy Hibbert, the home centre-forward, was then denied by a clever interception by Roberts, whose wonderful pass out to the left would have sent Wall away dangerously if Dewhurst had not upended him for a free-kick. Wall then reversed the play by hitting the ball over to the right to Meredith, whose shot seemed about to reach Sandy Turnbull in front of goal before James Raeside dashed out to grab the ball. United, however, had shown they could master the ball and the conditions and their supporters in the 29,500 crowd must have been heartened by their impressive start.

Ernest Mangnall's side continued to press and Raeside was forced to push away a shot from Wall, before Bury swept forward and Roberts showed the defensive side of his game by heading away a cross when the ball was swept into the United box. This marked the start of some considerable pressure from Bury, and it looked like they had made the breakthrough when Hibbert headed Gildea's cross past Moger, only to see the linesman's flag go up for offside. United were then similarly disappointed shortly afterwards when Roberts headed back Wall's corner, and when Meredith hit a hard shot James Turnbull's turning of the ball into the net brought the raising of the linesman's flag.

Wall then brought gasps of appreciation from the crowd when, advancing with the ball, he seemed to weave between Dewhurst and Jimmy Lindsey, only to let himself down by subsequently pushing the ball too far in front of the United forwards advancing towards the Bury goal. Lindsey was the only Bury player remaining from the famous FA Cup-winning side who had thrashed Derby 6–0 in 1903. The United left-winger, however, was having one of his best games for the club and for a while the ball seemed to be stuck to his foot, as pass after pass was directed in his direction. Lindsey would no doubt have liked to kick him out of the ground, but for a time he could not get near him to do so.

Considering how windy the conditions were the game was a fine, exciting affair. The away side were the more impressive but Bury were by no means out of the contest and when Stacey clattered into Hibbert there were some who felt Mr Horrocks, the referee from Bolton, might have given Bury a penalty. At half-time the score remained goalless.

Within seconds of the restart it really should have been 1–0 to the League leaders, when following a Hibbert miskick Roberts sent Wall away. When he pulled the ball back across the goal the United forwards seemed uncertain who should take it on and the chance was wasted. Wall then tried an effort of his own, the ball flashing past the 'keeper and narrowly wide. The left-wing man was not going to be denied for ever, and on the hour mark he got the goal that he, and his side, deserved. Bannister dashed through and when his shot was fumbled by the 'keeper Wall was swiftly on hand to knock the ball into the net. So it was 1–0 to United and with the wind in their favour it was a great position to be in, but within seconds of the restart Roberts was badly injured and had to be assisted from the field to receive treatment. Duckworth was asked to fill in for the centre-half with Bannister dropping to right-half. When United were forced to play with a man less for the remaining 30 minutes they did so without any serious problems, and when the referee blew the final whistle they had won a tough game 1–0 at the ground of one of their closest rivals for the Division One title. Nothing, it seemed, was going to stop United winning their first-ever Division One title.

Billy Hibbert

After only turning professional in 1906 at aged 22 the Bury centre-forward went on to have a long career in the game, just missing out on a century of goals at Gigg Lane before moving to Newcastle United in 1911, where he scored 46 goals either side of World War One. His later clubs included Bradford City and Oldham Athletic before he tried his luck playing for Fall River Marksmen in the American Soccer League, which had been established in 1921. He later took up a coaching career in the USA. Hibbert made one international appearance for England.

FA Cup First Round

Against: Blackpool (Home)

Date: Saturday 11 January 1908

Attendance: 11,747 (£352 receipts)

Result: Manchester United 3, Blackpool 1

Referee: F.H. Dennis of Middlesbrough.

Manchester United

Team: Moger, Holden, Stacey, Duckworth, McGillivray, Bell, Meredith, Bannister, J. Turnbull, A. Turnbull, Wall.

Scorers: Meredith, Wall (2)

Blackpool

Team: Fiske, Crewsdon, Scott, Threlfall, Parkinson, Connor, Gow, Haywood, W.A. Grundy, Weston, Brindley.

Scorer: Grundy

With Roberts unable to recover from his injury at Gigg Lane John McGillivray was brought in to make his debut for United. Otherwise the side for the first-round FA Cup game with Blackpool was the same as that which appeared at Bury. This was expected to be something of a stroll for the home side. Blackpool were in poor form and, although they had beaten near neighbours Oldham Athletic 1–0 at home on New Year's Day, the Seasiders were in 18th place (from 20) in Division Two. They had also failed to win away that season.

The match turned out to be a poor one for the crowd of just over 11,000. Wall, with two goals, was undoubtedly the star of the United forward line that might have scored a good few more except for a fine display by Bill Fiske in the Blackpool goal. Jack Scott at the back also worked tirelessly on an uncertain muddy pitch that was by no means perfect for good football. Although *The Manchester Evening News* reporter declared the experiment of playing McGillivray at centre-half a success, his view that 'he should make a capital understudy to Roberts' proved to be premature as the new man went on to make only another three appearances for the club.

Blackpool did, in fact, take the lead when on 20 minutes the amateur player W.A. Grundy scored from the right side of the penalty area with a shot that flew past Moger. When Sandy Turnbull was forced off the field shortly afterwards, and did not in fact subsequently play any part in the second half's proceedings, Blackpool's hopes must have been raised; however, they were to be dashed when Meredith, perhaps angered by a heavy challenge from Jack Parkinson that forced the referee to speak to the Blackpool man, hit a pacy shot from 20 yards that beat Fiske before cannoning off the post and into the net to make it 1–1.

Meredith's cross then found Wall, whose powerful shot Fiske could only help into the goal to ensure the home side ran off at half-time in front by two goals to one. Wall made it 3–1 when, from another Meredith cross, he managed to kick the ball past the 'keeper despite losing his footing.

League Match 22

Against: Sheffield United (Away)

Date: Saturday 18 January 1908

Attendance: 17,000

Result: Sheffield United 2, Manchester United 0

Referee: M.A. Green of West Bromwich.

Sheffield United   ⚽ ⚽

Team: Lievesley, Benson, Brookes, Wilkinson, North, Needham, Hobson, Hardinge, Brown, Batty, Lipsham.

Scorers: Batty, Wilkinson

Manchester United

Team: Moger, Holden, Burgess, Whiteside, McGillivray, Bell, Meredith, Bannister, J. Turnbull, Picken, Wall.

The match with Sheffield United was played at Bramall Lane, the ground which had hosted the world's first-ever floodlit football match on 14 October 1878 with two teams picked from the Sheffield Football Association. The power for the lights was provided by two generators.

Kerr Whiteside made his only first-team Manchester United appearance at Bramall Lane in January 1908, replacing Duckworth at right-half. With McGillivray making only his second appearance (and first in the League) at centre-half it was clearly going to be a difficult time for the former Scottish junior international signed from Irvine Victoria in May 1907.

For the home side there was a debut for James Hobson, signed from Worksop, and he must have feared the worst when one of his colleagues, Tommy North at centre-half, was hurt early on and was to be absent from the pitch for much of the following proceedings. With 10 men it was therefore all the more remarkable that a Sheffield side lying just three points outside the relegation zone became the first to beat the runaway leaders since their near neighbours The Wednesday had done so at the end of November.

Manchester United were unlucky not to take the lead in the first minute when Wall's shot came back into play from the crossbar. Then, with their first attack, Sheffield scored, Arthur Brown's powerful run leaving William Batty with a chance from 12 yards that Moger had no opportunity to save. When North was then carried off Brown was forced to drop to centre-half, from where he continued to pull the Manchester United defence to pieces with a series of darting runs and passes to his forwards.

The match appeared to have been decided when, following a corner-kick at the beginning of the second half, Willie Wilkinson hit a shot that Moger, with players in front of him, only saw once the ball had entered the net. This at last seemed to rouse the away team, and twice more Wall was unlucky when each time his shots struck the woodwork and flew away to safety. With Meredith, for once, kept quiet by the excellent Ernest Needham, the League leaders were unable to exert sufficient pressure on Joe Lievesley in goal to reduce the arrears, and when the game ended the home supporters in a 17,000 crowd were overjoyed.

There was sympathy in *The Manchester Evening News* for both Whiteside and McGillivray. The paper said 'It would be most unfair to blame the reserve men for the defeat', especially as Whiteside had clearly been injured early the second half, yet in comparison *The Sheffield Independent* felt that 'Roberts and Duckworth were badly missed', especially as Whiteside had been unable to give Meredith 'the sort of support which the famous right-winger is accustomed to receive from Duckworth.'

The result and performance had been a poor one for Ernest Mangnall. Wall, Holden and Moger in goal had all performed with distinction but that was not the case for the team, who, according to *The Sheffield Independent* had 'given little evidence of that greatness which has given them their proud position at the head of the League.'

Arthur Brown – youngest England international in the 20th century until Duncan Edwards

Centre-forward Arthur Brown was only 17 when he was signed by Sheffield United from Gainsborough Trinity in May 1902. A precocious talent, his main strengths were his opportunism in front of goal and a powerful, accurate shot. Earlier in the season he had scored four times against Sunderland at Bramall Lane.

Brown was capped before his 19th birthday in February 1904 and he remained the youngest England international in the 20th century until Duncan Edwards made his debut against Scotland on 2 April 1955 aged just 18 years and 183 days. Whereas Edwards went on to make another 17 international appearances Brown only played on one other occasion for his country. Brown was to leave Sheffield United at the end of the 1907–08 season, signing for Sunderland for a then world-record fee of £1,600.

League Match 23

Against: Chelsea (Home)

Date: Saturday 25 January 1908

Attendance: 20,000

Result: Manchester United 1, Chelsea 0

Manchester United

Team: Moger, Holden, Burgess, Downie, Roberts, Bell, Meredith, Picken, J. Turnbull, Menzies, Wall.

Scorer: J. Turnbull

Chelsea

Team: Whitley, Cameron, Miller, Key, McRoberts, Birnie, Brawn, Whitehouse, Hilsdon, Rouse, Fairgray.

Following the ease with which the Sheffield United forwards had run through the United half-back line the previous weekend, Ernest Mangnall was prepared to gamble by allowing Roberts, who had turned up expecting only to watch, to play in this match although he was clearly not fully fit. The manager needed a player like Roberts in the absence of some

Play up Newton Heath – postcard. Forerunners to Manchester United between 1878 to 1902.

Ten of the England side that played Scotland in 1905 including Ernie Roberts. The United captain would have played many more than three times for his country if not for the fact that he was one of staunchest supporters of the fledgling Players' Union.

Blackburn Rovers, pictured in 1906. Top row, left to right: Holmes (Trainer), Wolstenholm, Birchall, Wilson, Magill, Crompton, Cameron, Moir, R.B. Middleton. Middle row, left to right: Pentland, Whittaker, Smith, Davies, Bowman, McIver, Bradshaw. Bottom row, left to right: McAllister, Robertson, Evans, Chadwick, McClure.

The reigning champions at the start of the 1907–08 season were Newcastle United.

OPPOSITE THIS PLAQUE WAS THE
BANK STREET GROUND
HOME OF
MANCHESTER UNITED
FORMERLY NEWTON HEATH F.C.
1893 TO 1910

A plaque less than a mile from the City of Manchester Stadium is all that remains of Manchester United's stay at Bank Street, before their move to Old Trafford in 1910.

Bank Street. Looking across the Velodrome towards the City of Manchester Stadium.

This picture of Charlie Sagar scoring against Bristol City in 1905 gives some example of Bank Street in all its glory.

Robert Crompton of Blackburn Rovers. Rovers' greatest-ever player who held, with 41, the record for the most England International caps at the time. Described by the Sunderland and Arsenal legend Charlie Buchan as 'the finest footballer in the world before World War One'.

Steve Bloomer. One of the greatest players of his generation. A magnificent passer of the ball, he also possessed a powerful accurate shot, such that by the time he retired in 1914 he had rattled up 392 goals in 599 games for Derby and Middlesbrough, finishing as top scorer in the First Division on five separate occasions.

George Wall. A tricky left-winger whose ability to cut inside and shoot caught out many defences.

George Stacey. The full-back made his debut in October 1907 at St James' Park when Manchester United played one of their greatest games to defeat reigning League champions Newcastle United 6–1.

Andrew Wilson. Scotsman Andrew Wilson was a fine player who scored the Wednesday's consolation effort at Bank Street in March 1908 when his side suffered a 4–1 defeat at the hands of Ernest Mangnall's men.

Ernest Needham. The Sheffield United left-half was capped 16 times by England and in a long career won a Championship, two FA Cup-winners' and one losers' medal with his only club.

Bill Lyon. Angered at his booking in the final league game of the season, the Preston full-back refused to participate in the match until returning to score a free-kick with his first touch of the ball.

William Meredith cartoon.

Outcasts – both on and off the pitch, the Manchester United players of 1907–08 were determined to win their just rewards, and they formed the backbone of the campaign to establish a Players' Union.

The CHELSEA F.C. Chronicle

OFFICIAL PROGRAMME

of

The Chelsea Football & Athletic Company, Limited.

ENTERED AT STATIONERS' HALL.]

MEMBERS OF

The Football League (Division 1), South Eastern League (Division 1).

VOL. III. No. 36.]   Monday, April 27th, 1908.   [ONE PENNY.
POST FREE 1½d.

"FOR THE BEST CAUSE OF ALL."

Chelsea FC Chronicle cover, 1908.

QUEEN'S PARK RANGERS v. MANCHESTER UNITED.

FOOTBALL ASSOCIATION CHARITY SHIELD MATCH.

MONDAY, APRIL 27th, 1908.   *Kick-off 5.30 p.m.*

QUEEN'S PARK RANGERS (Green and White).

1
SHAW
Goal

2
MACDONALD
Right Back

3
FIDLER
Left Back

4
E. H. LINTOTT
Right Half

5
McLEAN
Centre Half

6
DOWNING
Left Half

7
PENTLAND
Outside Right

8
CANNON
Inside Right

9
P. G. SKILTON
Centre

10
GITTINS
Inside Left

11
BARNES
Outside Left

O

12
WALL
Outside Left

13
TURNBULL (J.)
Inside Left

14
TURNBULL (A.)
Centre

15
BANNISTER
Inside Right

16
MEREDITH
Outside Right

17
BELL
Left Half

18
ROBERTS
Centre Half

19
DOWNIE
Right Half

20
STACEY
Left Back

21
DUCKWORTH
Right Back

22
BROOMFIELD
Goal

MANCHESTER UNITED (Red).

Referee - - - - - Mr. J. T. HOWCROFT (Bolton).

Linesmen - - - - Messrs. G. W. SIMMONS (Herts) and M. T. ROBERTS (Derby).

ANY ALTERATIONS WILL BE NOTIFIED ON THE BOARD.

Printed and Published for the Proprietors (The Chelsea Football and Athletic Co., Ltd.), by JAS. TRUSCOTT & SON, LTD., London.

Charity Shield line-ups, 1908.

Football League champions.

key players. Firstly Duckworth had been ill during the week and it was felt unfair to play him knowing that on the Monday the United right-half was due to play for the North against the South in a match at Hyde Road and from which the England side to play Ireland in February would be selected. Up front Sandy Turnbull was unavailable after being suspended by the FA for one game as punishment for his sending off against Manchester City in December, and Bannister had to call off playing at the last moment owing to the death of his mother.

The manager decided that there was to be no second chance for Whiteside as there was a long-awaited return for Alex Downie, who had been a mainstay in the side until Duckworth had finally made the right-half position his own in the previous season. Jack Picken was selected as Bannister's replacement and Menzies played for Sandy Turnbull in a match that turned out to be his last of 25 first-team appearances for United.

Since the earlier fixture in the season at Stamford Bridge the Chelsea side had been strengthened by the signing of William Brawn from Middlesbrough for £950 in November.

The match was a very poor affair, one easily forgotten by the crowd of around 20,000, and afterwards *The Manchester Evening News* was especially critical of the forwards: 'Not one of the 10 players did himself justice, the six inside men* in particular being poor in the extreme. When Menzies changed places with Picken there was a big improvement, the only decent forward play of the match being seen during the last 15 minutes.'

It was during this time that the goal arrived when, with 10 minutes remaining, James Turnbull found himself unmarked with the ball at his feet and drove it past Jack Whitley. The Chelsea 'keeper might have been beaten earlier when the home side were awarded a penalty after John

'Jock' Cameron handled the ball, but Wall drove his shot straight at Whitley who saved easily.

*Inside men refers to inside-right centre-forward and inside-left.

Top of the table

Team	Played	Points
Man Utd	23	28
Newcastle Utd	25	31
The Wednesday	24	30
Bury	25	27
Man City	23	26

FA Cup Second Round

Against: Chelsea (Home)

Date: Saturday 1 February 1908

Attendance: 25,184

Result: Manchester United 1, Chelsea 0

Referee: F. Heath of Birmingham.

Manchester United

Team: Moger, Holden, Stacey, Duckworth, Roberts, Bell, Meredith, Bannister, J. Turnbull, A. Turnbull, Wall.

Scorer: A. Turnbull

Chelsea

Team: Whitley, Cameron, Miller, McRoberts, Stark, Birnie, Brawn, Rouse, Hilsdon, Windridge, Bridgeman.

Both sides arrived for this game after a week's special training at the seaside, Chelsea from Southport and United from Norbreck. The Londoners had beaten Midland League side Worksop Town 9–1 in the FA Cup first round, a result that remains the Pensioners' record victory in the FA Cup. George Hilsdon had scored six.

Ernest Mangnall was able to select Duckworth, Bannister and Sandy Turnbull to replace Downie, Picken and Menzies from the previous weekend's game.

The crowd, as was the FA Cup tradition that lasted well up to the late 1970s, was above average, with 5,000 more paying spectators present than for the League game between the same sides. Although the home team ended up going through to the next round, with Sandy Turnbull scoring the only goal of the game, they were fortunate to progress. Chelsea missed a late gilt-edged chance when Hilsdon hit his penalty wide in the 75th minute. It meant the Londoners were going to have to wait for their first FA Cup Final – seven years in fact, when they went down 3–0 to Sheffield United in 1915 at the start of World War One.

The game had sparked to life after just four minutes when Sandy Turnbull picked up the ball and from 25 yards hit a shot that deceived Whitley in the Chelsea goal. Stung by going behind, the away side had forced the pace for the rest of the half but had found Roberts back to his very best, blocking the Londoners' shots and relieving his beleaguered defence with some effective forward passes. It meant that at half-time Moger had hardly been tested, and that stayed the way even after Brawn went down under a Roberts challenge for a penalty with just 15 minutes remaining.

The home side were through to the third round of the FA Cup but it may have been that having already beaten Chelsea twice in the League that United were guilty of complacency as they rarely showed anything like their early-season form. There was criticism of a number of the players in *The Manchester Evening News* with Holden described as shaky, James Turnbull as showing 'too much desire to beat his opponents single-handed' and Wall as being 'most disappointing'.

League Match 24

Against: Newcastle United (Home)

Date: Saturday 8 February 1908

Attendance: 50,000

Result: Manchester United 1, Newcastle United 1

Manchester United

Team: Moger, Holden, Burgess, Duckworth, Downie, Bell, Meredith, Bannister, J. Turnbull, A. Turnbull, Wall.

Scorer: J. Turnbull

Newcastle United

Team: Lawrence, McCracken, Pudan, Gardner, Willis, McWilliam, Rutherford, Howie, Appleyard, Speedie, Ridley.

Scorer: Howie

The Manchester Evening News report on this match asked whether a 'better exhibition of football had ever been witnessed at Clayton.' Second-placed Newcastle must have known that defeat would spell the end of their chances of retaining the Division One title as before the match they had seven points fewer than the League leaders despite having played two more games. Having lost just once in their 16 previous League and Cup matches, Newcastle were determined to ensure there was no repeat of the St James' Park thumping earlier in the season.

A Bank Street record crowd watched the match, many of whom had gained entry for free by climbing in. After just six minutes the game had to be stopped when one section of the tightly-packed ground spilled over the barriers and on to the pitch. It was something of a miracle that the game ever reached its conclusion or that no one was seriously injured.

When the game restarted Manchester United pushed back the League champions. Downie, filling in for Roberts who had returned to the side too early after an injury, had a fine game at centre-half and was constantly finding his forwards with some wonderful passes. It was, however, Sandy Turnbull who was responsible for picking open the Newcastle defence for the opening goal. James Turnbull ran on to a delightful through ball and, with the Newcastle defenders appealing for off-side, got to the ball before Dick Pudan, who had advanced out of the penalty area, and fired it into the open net to the delight of the huge crowd. It might have been 2–0 at half-time but the United scorer was just too slow to react to a loose ball only seconds before the referee blew the whistle to end proceedings.

When the teams resumed it was clear that Newcastle were going to do everything in their powers to avoid defeat and if possible win the match. No side had so far even taken a single point away from Bank Street, could Newcastle be the first? An equaliser looked absolutely certain when Peter McWilliam was presented with the ball just six yards out, but with only Moger to beat he fired well wide for a poor miss.

By now the home side were constantly pressed back, but in Burgess they had the best player on the field and time after time he blocked the away side's forwards as they shaped to shoot.

With 10 minutes left it looked as if Manchester United were going to hang on for a famous victory, one that would put them well on course for a first-ever Division One title, but then Alex Gardner's free-kick to the back of the penalty area was headed back across by Bill Appleyard for Jimmy Howie to tap home and make it 1–1. With the home team on their knees it was not a question of whether they would suffer the loss of their first home point so far this season but whether they could hang on for a draw.

With five minutes of the match remaining Appleyard seemed to have the game won for Newcastle, brushing past Burgess and firing a low drive that Moger spilled. However, as the ball moved to roll over the line the 'keeper made a desperate recovering save to ensure a glorious game ended 1–1.

Although Burgess was the best player on display, Bell had also played magnificently. On the Newcastle side Joe Ridley's pace had been a constant threat, but all the forwards on both sides had played well.

'The team rose to the occasion in splendid fashion and every man is to be congratulated upon the part they played,' said *The Manchester Evening News*.

Bill McCracken

Belfast-born Bill McCracken was one of the most loathed footballers of his generation. This was as a result of his mastery of the offside trap, which when it was introduced in 1866 meant a player could be offside if there were fewer than three players between him and the opposing goalline when the ball was played.

Full-back McCracken, one of the game's thinkers, realised that a more effective way of stopping attacks than dispossessing the forwards was to move craftily up field at opportune times and catch them offside. McCracken so organised his defence that forwards were regularly caught offside. Although his tactics were seen as effective they were also viewed as unsporting and angered many opposing players and spectators.

The laws were changed in 1925, two years after McCracken retired at the end of a 19-year playing career with Newcastle in which he collected three League and one FA Cup-winners' medals. McCracken also represented Ireland and, following the partition of the country in 1921, Northern Ireland on 15 occasions, scoring a single goal.

Peter McWilliam

McWilliam played close to 250 games for Newcastle at left-half between 1902 and 1911, winning three League Championship medals in 1904–05, 1906–07 and 1908–09 and an FA Cup-winners' medal in 1910. After the war he managed Spurs to the Second Division title, and when the London side won the FA Cup the following season McWilliam became the first man to win the competition as a player and as a manager. McWilliam was capped eight times for Scotland.

New signings

In February 1908 Ernest Mangnall signed Joe Curry, a half-back from Scotswood FC, and Tommy Wilson, a forward from Leeds City. Curry was to make 14 first-team appearances in his career at Manchester United.

League Match 25 ——————

Against: Blackburn Rovers (Home)

Date: Saturday 15 February 1908

Attendance: 15,000

Result: Manchester United 1, Blackburn Rovers 2

Manchester United

Team: Moger, Holden, Burgess, Duckworth, Roberts, Bell, Meredith, Bannister, J. Turnbull, A. Turnbull, Wilson.

Scorer: A. Turnbull (pen)

Blackburn Rovers

Team: McIver, Heywood, Suttie, Walmsley, Stevenson, Houlker, Bracegirdle, Martin, Davies, Aitkenhead, Bradshaw.

Scorers: Aitkenhead, Davies

'Pulling the Lion's Tail'

On paper this was a racing certainty, United were unbeaten at home and had played a marvellous game the previous weekend. Rovers had not won away all season and when the teams had met earlier in the season had been thrashed 5–1 at home. They had also failed to win in 10 games and were lying in 19th place, just one off the bottom. To make matters worse the away side were also going to have to make do without their captain and best player Crompton, on duty for England against Ireland in Belfast for the opening match of the Home International Championship. This was a match the away side won 3–1.

Richard Duckworth, following his appearance in the North side against the South in January, had hoped to be playing in the international match but had been left disappointed by the selectors' decision to play Derby County's Ben Warren at right-half. The United right-half never did play for his country, although he did play five times for the Football League and was included on an FA tour party to South Africa in 1910. In this respect Duckworth would certainly challenge Steve Bruce for the winner of the 'best United half-back never to play for his country' award.

Of course, one of the great things about football is that it is not played on paper, and its history shows that even the lowliest can beat the mightiest on the day. So it was that the away side collected both points on offer in their best display of the season.

The match had been declared by the United committee as a benefit for two of the team's stalwarts, Bell, playing in the game, and Downie, who was not on display with Roberts back at centre-half. The two players would have much preferred the Sunderland, Chelsea or Newcastle game for such an occasion as the match was expected to attract fewer people than for those visits. This was, in fact, what happened with just 15,000 at Bank Street, and turnstile receipts of just £298, although fortunately for the pair United later obtained permission from the FA to increase the benefit money paid to each of them to £250.

With George Wall on international duty for England there was a debut for Tommy Wilson at left wing. It proved to be his only game for United.

The match was an odd affair with the home side enjoying the majority of possession and plenty of opportunities in front of goal. Yet at the end few of the 15,000 present would have begrudged a hard-working and talented Rovers side their victory, as after they took the lead they rarely looked like surrendering it. Only once was the away side's defence breached, and even that was from the penalty spot.

Walter Aitkenhead had put Blackburn into the lead in the 20th minute when Billy Bradshaw broke forward and on a pitch covered with water in parts was able to get to the byline before crossing to find Aitkenhead. The Blackburn lead was doubled just a minute into the second half when, after John Martin, Ernest Bracegirdle and Bill Davies linked up, the last named beat Moger with a crisp shot. United got back into the game when, following a handling offence by Albert Walmsley in the 75th minute, Sandy Turnbull struck the resulting penalty past Willie McIver. The 'keeper was determined not to be beaten again and twice in the last 10 minutes he made outstanding saves to deny both James and Sandy Turnbull.

The result allowed Rovers to move out of the relegation zone, but with Newcastle able only to draw at home to Manchester City and third-placed The Wednesday heavily beaten by Aston Villa it meant United's lead at the top remained a healthy six points with two games in hand. The result was a little reminder, however, that the League trophy was not yet at Bank Street.

Home International Championship

The Home International Championship was football's oldest international series and had been contested annually between England, Scotland, Wales and all Ireland (later Northern Ireland following independence in the south in the 1920s) since 1883–84.

Scotland won the first series and it was not until 1887—88 that England replaced them as winners. Wales notched their first Championship in 1906—07, but at the start of the 1908 Championship Ireland had yet to register their first success (they were to do so in 1914).

The British Championship came to an end in 1984 when both England and Scotland announced their withdrawal from future competitions, citing waning interest, crowded international fixture lists and the hooliganism that increasingly accompanied many of the games. With each side taking three points from a record of won one, drawn one and lost one, Northern Ireland took the final Championship on goal difference. Since 1984 there have been a number of attempts to revive the tournament but the FA have made clear they have no intention of entering a team, making the idea redundant.

FA Cup Third Round

Against: Aston Villa (Away)

Date: Saturday 22 February 1908

Attendance: 12,777

Result: Aston Villa 0, Manchester United 2

Aston Villa

Team: George, Lyons, Miles, Tranter, J. Logan, Codling, Wallace, Cantrell, Garraty, Bache, Hall.

Manchester United

Team: Moger, Stacey, Holden, Burgess, Roberts, Bell, Meredith, Bannister, Berry, A. Turnbull, Wall.

Scorers: Wall, A. Turnbull

William 'Bill' Berry made his United debut at Hillsborough in January 1906, but it was not a happy occasion as Sheffield Wednesday won 5–2. He was to make 13 First Division appearances and this one FA Cup appearance at Villa Park, in which Ernest Mangnall's side moved within two matches of a first-ever FA Cup Final after a hard-fought tussle ended the home side's hopes of moving towards a fifth FA Cup success after victories in 1887, 1895, 1897 and 1905.

There was a blow to Aston Villa's chances before kick-off when Harry Hampton was declared unfit. A deadly goalscorer, Hampton could be relied on to barge both 'keeper and ball into the net if given the opportunity to do so.

Despite the loss of their chief assassin it was Aston Villa who began the match in confident style, pressing United back for the first quarter of an hour, but before half-time the contest was largely over after some superb wing play from Meredith and his colleague Wall on the left. It would have been difficult enough for any defence to hold one on their day, but when both were in peak form no team in England at the time could possibly have stopped them – and certainly not Aston Villa!

It was Wall who opened the scoring on the half-hour mark, drifting from his left-wing position into the inside-right area to collect Duckworth's pass and finish with some style from just outside the penalty area. It was a good goal, but the one that followed from Sandy Turnbull was an even better one, the United inside-left half-volleying another pass from Duckworth to leave Villa 'keeper Billy George helpless. Villa fans had been in boisterous fashion when their side had pressed, but after the United goals their silence for the remainder of the game was an obvious sign that they realised their side were not going to make a comeback. Early in the second period Bannister appeared to have made it 3–0, only to see his effort ruled out for offside. In the end it did not matter, as when the referee ended the contest United had beaten the Villians on their own ground in the FA Cup third round for the second time in three seasons, having sensationally knocked the then Cup holders out in February 1906 by a remarkable scoreline of 5–1.

The Manchester Evening News was afterwards full of praise for a 'Fine Performance by Manchester United', stating 'Considering the fact that a gale blew throughout, the passing of the United men was remarkable and their footwork at times simply bewildered the opposing defence. [...] rarely a pass went astray and there was not a weak spot on the side. The forwards worked splendidly together, and the halves played well to a man. Stacey proved what a useful player he is, filling Holden's place equally as well as he did that of Burgess in recent games.'

With the Championship almost guaranteed the question on the club's followers' lips was: could Manchester United do the double of winning the League and FA Cup as achieved by Preston North End in 1888–89 and Aston Villa in 1896–97?

When the quarter-final draw was made United found themselves waiting to see who won a replay at Craven Cottage after Fulham had drawn 1–1 with Manchester City at Hyde Road. The Cottagers proved successful, winning 3–1, giving United an away tie against a side enjoying their first season of League football after gaining admission to the Football League after winning the Southern League in 1905–06 and 1906–07.

League Match 26

Against: Birmingham (Home)

Date: Saturday 29 February 1908

Attendance: 12,000

Result: Manchester United 1, Birmingham 0

Referee: T. Armitt of Leek.

Manchester United

Team: Moger, Holden, Stacey, Duckworth, Roberts, Bell, Meredith, Bannister, J. Turnbull, A. Turnbull, Wall.

Scorer: A. Turnbull

Birmingham

Team: Dorrington, Kearns, Stokes, Green, Wigmore, Cornan, Peplow, Montgomery, W.L. Jones, Drake, Eyre.

Although United maintained their dominance at the top of the table by defeating Birmingham ('City' not being added until 1943), they did so with what was one of their poorest performances of the season so far. It may have been that the team's attentions were on the match planned for Craven Cottage the following weekend, but Ernest Mangnall's side appeared lethargic and a better side than Birmingham would surely have taken advantage to gain at least a point. It would have been a valuable one too, as Birmingham arrived in the relegation zone with just 22 points from 26 matches.

The game was played on a heavy pitch following a week in which snow had fallen heavily and was now melting due to a strong sun. Burgess was absent from the United side and Charlie Tickle was absent from the away side. They were both playing for the Football League against the Scottish League at Birmingham's St Andrew's ground that afternoon – a match won by the home side 2–0 with goals from Warren and Hilsdon.

The only goal at Bank Street came when a good many spectators were entering the ground. A neat bout of passing between the Turnbulls resulted in Sandy scoring a fine goal from a narrow angle. His colleague James then slipped when put clean through shortly afterwards.

Meredith was left fuming when he was dumped on the floor by Benny Green, and when both players squared up to each other the referee Mr Armitt from Leek spoke to them. By the time Holden and Ninty Eyre were injured going for the same ball the pitch had made passing almost impossible, and the second half turned out to be one long slog that would have done little to warm any of the watching crowd.

Jack Dorrington had a fine game in goal for the West Midlands side but up front, reported *The Manchester Evening News*, they 'were practically useless, Moger having very few shots to deal with.' Roberts and Bannister, who worked hard, were regarded as the best players on the field, but there was bad news for Holden who limped off towards the end with a bad knee injury and was rated as being unlikely to play again for a number of weeks.

In fact, Richard Holden had played his final game of the season, and although he eventually recovered he was never quite the same player. Fortunately, his 26 League appearances meant he received a League-winners' medal at the season's end, something denied to him when United again won the League in 1910–11 as during that campaign he made only eight League appearances. His injury presented an opportunity for George Stacey to cement his place in the starting line up.

Victory against Birmingham took United eight points clear at the top, knowing that victory the following weekend would take them within touching distance of the double. Birmingham crashed to the bottom of the table, where they were to remain to the season's end.

FA Cup Fourth Round

Against: Fulham (Away)

Date: Saturday 7 March 1908

Attendance: 41,000

Result: Fulham 2, Manchester United 1

Referee: T. Kirkham of Burslem.

Fulham

Team: Skene, Ross, Lindsay, Collins, Morrison, Geldie, McHughton, Dalrymple, Harrison, Fraser, Mouncher.

Scorer: Harrison (2)

Manchester United

Team: Moger, Stacey, Burgess, Duckworth, Roberts, Bell, Meredith, Bannister, J. Turnbull, A. Turnbull, Wall.

Scorer: J. Turnbull

Having never previously even reached the last eight, Fulham created a minor sensation when the Second Division side knocked United out of the 1908 FA Cup to advance to play Newcastle United in the semi-final. And while Bill Harrison with his two goals was undoubtedly the hero of the hour for the Cottagers, it was the Londoners' defence which was the major factor in their victory. Leslie Skene, in particular, had a memorable game between the posts, showing some extraordinary goalkeeping skills in the first half especially, while in the second he was grateful to his half-back line up in front who worked tirelessly to prevent the away side creating the chances to at least force a draw. At the same time Fulham also enjoyed a degree of luck, which any side needs if they are to go on and win the FA Cup, when Skene appeared to catch a header from Sandy Turnbull after it had crossed the line and when Bannister's shot hit the 'keeper's legs and went behind for a corner. Fulham's opening goal was also fortunate when an attempted clearance by Burgess saw the ball cannon off Harrison and past Moger into the net in the 11th minute.

Harrison, along with Bob Dalrymple and Fred Mouncher, was a constant threat to Duckworth, Bell and Roberts. The League leaders had equalised when on 56 minutes Meredith seemed to be taking the ball out of play, but when he hooked it back Sandy Turnbull headed it across the goal for James Turnbull to turn the ball home.

The winning goal came in the 65th minute when Moger was unable to prevent Harrison's shot entering the net despite getting a hand to the ball. The Fulham man could have had a hat-trick shortly afterwards if Burgess had not rescued his side with a sliding tackle as he shaped to shoot.

As the game moved towards its conclusion James Turnbull seemed certain to equalise and force the tie to a replay but Archie Lindsay, straining every muscle, hooked his shot over the bar, and in the last few minutes amid great excitement Fulham hung on amid intense pressure to send their supporters home ecstatic.

The game was probably the finest that Craven Cottage had then witnessed, and although the rewards for success could not have been greater the match itself was played in a sporting manner that did credit to both sides. United may have lost but they emerged with their reputation intact.

Fulham supporters' hopes of winning the FA Cup were dashed in the semi-final, however, when Newcastle United recorded a still-to-be-broken record semi-final victory of six goals to nil, the Geordies moving forward to play another Division Two side in Wolverhampton Wanderers in the Final. Fulham ended the season missing out on promotion by three points. It was not until 1949 that Craven Cottage witnessed First Division football and not until 1975 did the Cottagers finally reach the FA Cup Final.

League Match 27

Against: Sunderland (Home)

Date: Saturday 14 March 1908

Attendance: 10,000

Result: Manchester United 3, Sunderland 0

‹ Manchester United ⚽ ⚽ ⚽

Team: Moger, Stacey, Burgess, Duckworth, Roberts, Bell, Meredith, Bannister, Berry, A. Turnbull, Wall.

Scorers: Bell, Berry (only goal for club), Wall

Sunderland

Team: Roose, Marples, Foster, Daykin, Low, Jarvie, Thompson, Hogg, Raybould, Holley, Bridgett.

With only two points separating them from the bottom two, Sunderland must have travelled to Bank Street fearing the worst. The Wearsiders had, however, recorded their biggest success of the season the previous weekend, winning 7–2 at Roker Park against Nottingham Forest to make it four wins in seven since Leigh Richmond Roose had made his debut in goal after signing from Stoke City.

Roose, whose amateur status allowed him to move between clubs, was a colleague of Meredith's in the Welsh national team, making his debut for Wales in a 2–0 defeat of Ireland in 1900 and ending up with 24 caps following his final game against Scotland in 1911. Along with Meredith, Roose was one of Wales' key players when the team won the Home International Championship for the first time in 1907. The 'keeper had played for his country the previous weekend when they had gone down 2–1 to Scotland after taking the lead through William 'Lot' Jones. Wales had been denied the services of Meredith after the Manchester United committee, in the light of the FA Cup match, had refused to allow him to play. English clubs at the time would often refuse to release Irish, Scots or Welsh players to play for their countries but could not deny English players the chance as FA rules forbade it. Both Roose and Meredith were set to play for their country on the following Monday at the Racecourse Ground against England.

Standing 6ft 1in tall and weighing over 13 stone, Roose was perfectly built to meet the robust strikers of the period on equal terms – comparisons to Peter Schmeichel in more modern times would not be inappropriate, especially as Roose was also well known for saving penalties. Roose was also noted for taking advantage of the laws in 1907–08 that allowed the goalkeeper to handle the ball anywhere in his own half. It has been said that the 1912 laws alteration whereby a 'keeper was forbidden to handle outside the penalty area was due to Roose's performances. Roose later played for Aston Villa and Arsenal but was killed at the Battle of the Somme during World War One in 1916. His body was never recovered and he is listed on the war memorial to missing soldiers at Thiepval.

Match report from *The Newcastle Daily Chronicle*:

MANCHESTER UNITED 3
SUNDERLAND 0
(Bell, Berry, Wall)

Referee: Mr J.Mason of Burslem
Attendance: 10,000

This result came as no surprise to Sunderland supporters who had not dared to hope for more than a draw. But the League leaders are a hard nut to crack and Sunderland's efforts to avenge their earlier defeat this season at the hands of United proved futile. Dame fortune was against Sunderland in several ways. Daykin had to be

---

carried off the field after 15 minutes after being hurt in a collision with Bell and for the remainder of the game Sunderland played with 10 men.

The Manchester public did not patronise the game and there were barely 10,000 people at Clayton. No doubt the treacherous weather was to blame, as was the expectation of an easy victory for the League leaders. Berry replaced Turnbull, who was still feeling the effects of an injury at centre-forward for United. Berry kicked-off and Sunderland launched the first attack. Fine enthusiasm or perhaps desperation was exhibited by the forwards, who quickly took advantage of a miskick by Wall.

Thompson and Bridgett had a fine understanding and Bridgett directed the first shot at the United goal. It was very forceful but Moger managed to save. The ball remained uncomfortably close to his goal and the home side had Burgess to thank for saving a certain goal by coolly heading out a fast, close-range shot. After the home custodian had cleared a corner United's front line got into businesslike mood. Berry sent in a dangerous centre and had Roose not been vigilant and active Turnbull's header would surely have found the net.

Roose saved from Wall and then Bridgett and Holley threatened the home citadel. They did not meet with success because of the excellent performance of Burgess and Stacey who were kept busy. Seesaw movements followed in which Meredith's pertinacity was very noticeable. Raybould neatly beat Stacey and put Bridgett in possession. He raced clear but sent his shot a good deal too high. Marples cleared cleverly when danger threatened, only for Turnbull to wriggle through brilliantly only to fail at the last.

The home defence were being given a tough time. Thompson centred well but Stacey, Duckworth and Roberts put in some magnificent work, with one clearance by Duckworth being outstanding. Sunderland were playing grandly and evoked applause from the crowd on several occasions. Burgess whipped the ball off the toes of Raybould as he was making a headlong dash for goal. But it was obvious that the loss of Daykin was making matters difficult for Sunderland.

Stacey was too good for Bridgett and played the ball to Wall who put Meredith in possession. He beat Foster and centred for Marples to clear splendidly. Turnbull and Meredith were giving a grand display and it was Meredith who created the first goal scored by Bel,l who gave Roose no chance. United maintained the pressure and Roose proved his worth as the home side showed distinct superiority in the closing stages of the first half. Berry scored United's second goal and again Roose had no chance.

On the restart United were aggressive and promptly forced a corner that Roose fisted away. Bridgett got away in his familiar style and centred to Holley, who gave Moger some difficulty with the save. United's third goal was not long in coming when Wall received from Berry and centred. Turnbull shot for goal and Roose had hardly got the ball away when Wall latched onto it again and banged it into the net. With a weakened team Sunderland could make little headway after that.

Bridgett and his teammates made strenuous efforts to remedy things but all in vain. For a time it seemed to be a contest between United's forwards and Roose, who was holding his own manfully.

Home International Championship

Date: 14 March 1908

Venue: Dalymount Park, Dublin

Result: Ireland 0 Scotland 5

Scorers: Jimmy Quinn (4), James Galt

Game featuring the first substitute in British football

Date: 16 March 1908

Venue: Racecourse Ground, Wrexham

Result: Wales 1 England 7

Wales' defence of their title came to an inglorious end as England set themselves up for a last-day decider with Scotland after both sides had won their games against Ireland and Wales, who would now fight to avoid being given the 'wooden spoon' for finishing bottom of the table.

The match was played on a foggy, muddy day. Within minutes Roose suffered a heavy injury when he dived bravely as the feet of the onrushing England forwards, and in the scrimmage that followed the 'keeper was kicked unconscious. To make matters worse, as he was being revived and carried from the field of play Nottingham Forest's Edwin Hughes also had to be escorted off, the decision to play him, despite feeling unwell, clearly being a poor one. Wales were thus down to nine men in the ninth minute and within a minute of going in goal Grenville Morris had conceded the first. Roose was then seen limping back on to the field, but heroically as he then performed it was soon 2–0 and he was dragged from the field after collapsing. At half-time it was 4–0 and with just nine men Wales were set to be routed.

It was then that Mr C.J. Hughes, one of the FA's VIPs who was in charge of the England players, entered the press box and informed the reporters that he had suggested allowing Wales be permitted a substitute 'keeper. This was an entire novelty as far as British Football was concerned, although in America at the time injured players could be replaced. So on 49 minutes Wrexham's Dai Davies emerged to play the rest of the match, which ended with England winning 7–1. Billy Meredith had played for Wales but his side never had a chance of winning the game.

Manchester Cup

Against: Manchester City (Home)

Date: Wednesday 18 March 1908

Result: Manchester United 1 Manchester City 0

Wall (penalty)

With Moger's run of 75 consecutive games coming to an end there was a debut from Broomfield in a match that would have disappointed the crowd, who despite promises by both managers beforehand saw two sides with five reserve players in each. The home side won with a Wall penalty given against Jackman for a foul on Berry.

League Match 28

Against: Woolwich Arsenal (Away)

Date: Saturday 21 March 1908

Attendance: 20,000

Result: Woolwich Arsenal 1, Manchester United 0

Referee: Mr Hayes of Nottingham.

Woolwich Arsenal

Team: Ashcroft, Gray, Sharp, Ducat, Sands, McEachrane, Lee, Davis, C. Satterthwaite, J. Satterthwaite, Neave.

Scorer: Lee

Manchester United

Team: Broomfield, Stacey, Burgess, Duckworth, Roberts, Bell, Meredith, Bannister, Berry, Picken, Wall.

Broomfield made his League debut in place of Moger, still missing due to blood poisoning in his finger. The new 'keeper had to be down smartly to save a Charlie Lewis shot as Arsenal showed their intent in the first minute.

Arsenal had been founded in 1886 and were the first Southern club to join the Football League, in 1893. For the majority of their time in southeast London, Arsenal played at the Manor Ground in Plumstead, a three-year period at the nearby Invicta Ground between 1890 and 1893 excepted. The Manor Ground was initially just a field, until the club installed stands and terracing in time for their first Football League match in September 1893. They played their home games there for the next 20 years until they moved permanently to north London in 1913, when Woolwich was dropped from the club's name.

The Arsenal manager Phil Kelso had clearly urged his players to get forward and Lewis, David Neave and Harold Lee then all forced Broomfield into decent saves before the United side, through Bannister, finally forced their first effort on goal. This appeared to inspire the away team as they then dominated the rest of the first half, Wall beating the Arsenal defence for pace only to shoot narrowly wide, when he might on another day have scored, and at half-time the game remained deadlocked at 0–0.

Within seconds of the restart a driving run by Meredith, perhaps his only real contribution all afternoon, ended unluckily for the Welshman when his shot was kicked away from the line by Andy Ducat with Ashcroft beaten – clearly this was not going to be Meredith's week! Arsenal, too, were unlucky when Charlie Satterthwaite, who had helped Liverpool win their first First Division League title in the 1900–01 season, hit the crossbar, and amazingly when it rebounded Lewis somehow hooked the ball over the bar from just three yards out.

With the game by now seemingly set to end in a draw Woolwich Arsenal managed one final attack when from a Neave pass across the field Lee headed the ball into the net amid tremendous enthusiasm from the home spectators in an above-average-size crowd.

When the referee sounded his final whistle victory had gone to the harder working, more determined outfit on the day, and although the away side were still well in front in the League a return of seven points from the last seven League games was much poorer than in the early part of the season.

League Match 29

Against: Liverpool (Away)

Date: Wednesday 25 March 1908

Attendance: 10,000

Result: Liverpool 7, Manchester United 4

Liverpool ✪✪✪✪✪✪✪

Team: Doig, West, Saul, Harrop, Raisbeck, Chorlton, Goddard, Robinson, J. Hewitt, McPherson, Cox.

Scorers: J. Hewitt (2), McPherson (3), Robinson (2)

Manchester United ✪✪✪✪

Team: Moger, Stacey, Dalton, Duckworth, Roberts, Downie, Meredith, Bannister, J. Turnbull, Picken, Wall.

Scorers: Wall (2), J. Turnbull, Bannister

Having easily beaten Liverpool at home in September, and also recorded their first-ever victory at Anfield courtesy of a single Sandy Turnbull goal at the end of the previous season, table-topping United were intent in making it three wins in a row against a Liverpool side back in 12th place, 14 points behind the leaders. The Scousers had also lost five games at home including their previous match 1–0 against Manchester City.

Not for the last time in matches between Liverpool and United, the form book was torn apart. But so was the United defence, especially in the first half. The match had originally been planned to take place in January but frost had caused its cancellation. As a result, with no such thing as floodlights for another 50 years or so, the game took place in the middle of a working day, cutting the size of the crowd substantially to just 10,000. Ted Dalton was given his debut for Manchester United, replacing the injured Burgess, while there were also appearances for Downie and Picken as replacements for Bell and Sandy Turnbull. Liverpool were also forced to field a weakened side with Hardy, out through a knee injury, Maurice Parry and James Bradley's places taken by Ted Doig, Thomas Chorlton and James Harrop respectively.

The small crowd witnessed an exciting match in which it took only three minutes for Liverpool to take the lead, Joe Hewitt fastening on to a centre from Goddard to crash home a magnificent shot that caught the underside of the bar before flying into the net. Nine minutes later Billy McPherson was on to another Arthur Goddard centre to make it two, Robbie Robinson then knocked home a Jack Cox cross for 3–0 before McPherson drilled in the fourth on the stroke of half-time. Already Manchester United had conceded more goals in 45 minutes than in the whole of 90 minutes in any other game that season. Back in 1895 Liverpool had battered Newton Heath 7–1, could they equal or even better this in 1908?

Doig, however, gave the away side a lifeline at the start of the second period, dropping a Roberts free-kick to a grateful Wall to make it 4–1 and then miskicking to present the United outside-left with his and his side's second. So it was 4–2 – was a famous comeback now on? When McPherson made it 5–2 the answer was no, especially as Robinson then made it 6–2! However, the away side were determined to go down fighting, and despite being four goals down they pinned the home side back around their penalty area with

Turnbull and Bannister reducing the arrears to 6–4 with quarter of an hour left. It was now a game from which no spectator could take his eyes away. Doig made a marvellous save from Meredith as United pressed, before Hewitt, who had been outstanding, finally ended any doubts about who would win by making it 7–4. When the final whistle sounded 'the enthusiasm equalled anything seen on the ground for many a long day. Absentees may think United were not trying too hard; they were' reported *The Football Field*. It had been a truly marvellous match, one which must go down as one of the finest ever between the sides.

Top of the table

Team	Played	Points
Man Utd	29	43
Newcastle Utd	31	38
The Wednesday	30	36
Man City	30	34

Joe Hewitt

When Liverpool had won the League in 1905–06 Hewitt had scored 23 goals in 37 appearances, and after missing most of the next was back to his rampaging best in the 1907–08 season, ending up with 21 goals.

Arthur Goddard

By the time he left Liverpool in 1914 Goddard had made over 400 appearances, mainly on the right wing. He often skippered the side and was known as 'Graceful Artie' by home fans for the stylish way he played the game. He scored 80 times for Liverpool.

League Match 30

Against: The Wednesday (Home)

Date: Saturday 28 March 1908

Result: Manchester United 4, The Wednesday 1

Referee: Mr J.H. Pearson of Crewe.

Manchester United   ⚽ ⚽ ⚽ ⚽

Team: Broomfield, Stacey, Burgess, Duckworth, Downie, Bell, Meredith, Bannister, Halse, A. Turnbull, Wall.

Scorers: Halse, Wall (2), A. Turnbull

The Wednesday   ⚽

Team: Lyall, Layton, Slavin, Brittleton, Miller, Bartlett, Maxwell, Bradshaw, Wilson, Stewart, Simpson.

Scorer: Wilson

This was a match The Wednesday had to win if they were to have any chance of overturning United's lead at the top of the table, but after consecutive defeats there was never really the prospect of a third for Ernest Mangnall's side after they raced into the lead in the first minute.

The goalscorer was debutant Harold Halse, signed for £350 from Southern League side Southend United after scoring 200 goals for the Shrimpers and in the side for James Turnbull. It was to be the first of 56 goals that Halse was to score for United in 123 League and Cup appearances until he signed for Aston Villa in the summer of 1912. It may have also been his luckiest as it came when Walter Miller, the Wednesday centre-half, in attempting to clear Halse's first shot, hit the ball off the United man only to see it loop over Jack Lyall, whose frantic efforts to retrieve the ball were in vain.

Any hopes that this might be the start of a thrilling game were swiftly stifled with both sides having trouble in controlling the ball in windy, sunny conditions. Halse might have scored a second but with both defences well on top it was no great surprise that at half-time the score was still 1–0.

Broomfield saved smartly when Andrew Wilson shot towards goal in the second minute of the second half, and when the ball spun away it seemed certain to end up in the goal, but Duckworth timed his sliding run to perfection to clear just as Jimmy Stewart looked to prod home. A goal then might have made it an interesting game but on 55 minutes United doubled their lead when, following a neat interchange of passes down the right, Meredith pulled the ball back only for Bannister to totally miss the ball. However, when the Wednesday defenders failed to clear properly, Meredith again crossed and this time Wall made no mistake.

Stewart was unlucky not to reduce the arrears when his shot cannoned back into play off the foot of the post before Wilson beat Broomfield with a fine shot to make it 2–1. The away side's hopes, now raised, were soon extinguished when within minutes Sandy Turnbull was left unmarked to score, and then Wall outpaced Willie Layton to run on and beat Lyall with a well-placed shot to put the home side 4–1 up, which was how it finished at the end of the 90 minutes.

The result meant that with Newcastle United otherwise occupied thrashing Fulham in the FA Cup semi-final, United's lead at the top of the table rose to seven points with a game in hand. Eight points from eight games would be enough for Mangnall's men to win the title.

Team	Played	Points
Man Utd	30	45
Newcastle Utd	31	38
The Wednesday	31	36
Man City	31	36

Arthur Dickinson

Dickinson, the Wednesday manager in 1907, remains the club's longest serving and most successful boss with 393 wins, 338 losses and 188 draws in 919 games with the club. He also managed the club to two League titles and two FA Cups during his 29-year reign.

League Match 31

Against: Bristol City (Away)

Date: Saturday 4 April 1908

Attendance: 12,000

Result: Bristol City 1, Manchester United 1

Referee: J.H. Pearson of Crewe.

Bristol City

Team: Clay, Annan, Cottle, Spear, Gilligan, Hanlin, Maxwell, Staniforth, Rippon, Burton, Hilton.

Scorer: Maxwell

Manchester United   ⚽

Team: Broomfield, Stacey, Burgess, Duckworth, Roberts, Bell, Meredith, Bannister, Halse, A. Turnbull, Wall.

Scorer: Wall

United's opponents were in the middle of a dreadful run that unless halted seemed certain to return them to Division Two after just two seasons of top-flight football. Since New Year's Day Bristol had played 12 League games, winning just one and drawing three, leaving them just two points clear of the relegation zone. The home side were also missing Billy Wedlock who was playing that day for England at Hampden Park in the Home International Championship deciding match against Scotland. Wedlock had been selected, as on many other occasions, in preference to Charlie Roberts, to play centre-half for England.

When the Home International ended 1–1, with Chelsea's Jimmy Windridge equalising a first-half goal by The Wednesday's Andy Wilson for the home side, it meant that the title was shared. The match was lucky to finish as too many people had been allowed in, the attendance of 121,452 being a world record at the time. Only the intervention of the police kept the pitch clear. It appeared that the football authorities had failed to learn the lessons of 1902 when 25 fans had died when parts of a stand had collapsed during a Scotland vs England game played at Ibrox, home of Glasgow Rangers. With Ireland later beating Wales in the final match the Welsh had gone from top to bottom in a year.

At Bristol City Sammy Gilligan replaced Wedlock at centre-half for the visit of the League leaders, and after Harry Clay fisted away Meredith's shot the home side were unlucky when William Maxwell's shot hit the upright.

Manchester United's good fortune continued when Stacey appeared to handle the ball in the area from another Maxwell effort. Pat Hanlin's tussle with Meredith was one of the highlights of the game but just before the break the Welshman finally broke clear, and when he crossed Wall hit a powerful shot that entered the net off the crossbar to give United a 1–0 lead.

In the second period the home side appeared to have little likelihood of forcing themselves back into the game, especially as United now had the advantage of kicking with a stiff breeze behind them. Meredith missed narrowly on two occasions before Halse's long-range shot hit the bar.

It seemed only a matter of time before it became 2–0, but with 20 minutes left Maxwell struck the equaliser following a mix-up in the United defence. Both sides might have welcomed a point beforehand, City to keep them out of the bottom two and a stuttering United, whose 1907 sparkling form had long since given way to ragged, hotchpotch performances, because it moved them a point nearer the title. The away side had not been helped by the absence of James Turnbull at centre-forward, where Halse's inexperience was naturally showing.

In a poor game *The Manchester Courier* made Meredith the best United forward, but felt that only Broomfield and Roberts had played up to their reputation. Gilligan, who took Wedlock's place, was praised as well as centre-forward Willis Rippon on the home side.

Top of the table

Team	Played	Points
Man Utd	31	46
The Wednesday	32	38
Newcastle Utd	33	38
Man City	32	36

League Match 32

Against: Everton (Away)

Date: Wednesday 8 April 1908

Attendance: 17,000

Result: Everton 1, Manchester United 3

Everton ⚽

Team: Scott, W. Balmer, Maconnachie, Makepeace, Taylor, Adamson, Rafferty, Coleman, A. Young, J. Settle, Donnachie.

Scorer: Young

Manchester United ⚽ ⚽ ⚽

Team: Broomfield, Stacey, Burgess, Duckworth, Roberts, Downie, Meredith, Bannister, Halse, A. Turnbull, Wall.

Scorers: Halse, A. Turnbull (pen), Wall

When it became apparent that both Newcastle United and The Wedneday had lost to Aston Villa and Middlesbrough respectively, it meant that by winning at Goodison Park Manchester United had to all intents and purposes captured the First Division trophy for the first time in the club's history. It was true that either, or both, Manchester City or the side from Sheffield could have won all five of their remaining games to end up level on points with United, but that would also have meant Ernest Mangnall's men would have to lose their remaining six fixtures. It was now just a matter of when the title would be confirmed, not if.

It may have been this which inspired United when Everton equalised in the 67th minute of the match at Goodison Park, Joe Donnachie beating Duckworth and Stacey before drawing Broomfield and squaring the ball for Alex Young to complete the formalities by prodding the ball into an empty net.

Having dominated their opponents the injustice of conceding a goal saw the away side pour forward, and when Sandy Turnbull's shot was handled by Walter Balmer the United inside-left thrashed home the penalty to the joy of a small handful of the side's supporters who had been able to make the trip for the midweek afternoon fixture.

Halse, who was again preferred to James Turnbull at centre-forward, had given his side the lead in the first half, surprising Billy Scott with a curling shot. It was Wall who added the third in the final minute, hammering home a shot that the Everton 'keeper probably never even saw.

Meredith, Turnbull and Wall had all played magnificently, but this was a fine all-round team performance at the end of which United rightly earned the applause of the crowd.

Other key fixtures

Date: Monday 6 April
Result: Man City 5, Preston 0

Date: Wednesday 8 April
Result: Middlesbrough 6, The Wednesday 1

Result: Newcastle Utd 2, Aston Villa 5

Top of the table

Team	Played	Points
Man Utd	32	48
Newcastle Utd	34	38
The Wednesday	33	38
Man City	33	38

League Match 33

Against: Notts County (Home)

Date: Saturday 11 April 1908

Attendance: 20,000

Result: Manchester United 0, Notts County 1

Referee: C.C. Fallowfield of Lincoln.

Manchester United

Team: Broomfield, Stacey, Burgess, Duckworth, Downie, Bell, Berry, Bannister, J. Turnbull, A. Turnbull, Wall.

Notts County

Team: Iremonger, Morley, Montgomery, Griffiths, Clamp, Craythorne, Harper, Matthews, Gooch, Cantrell, Dodd.

Scorer: Dodd

Despite being assured of a first-ever League Championship trophy, the Bank Street crowd were outraged at the United performance. Notts County were fighting for survival but had a more than decent defence so a hard game was assured.

Before the match it had been announced that the move to the proposed new stadium in Stretford had now been agreed. While undoubtedly a sign of the club's development, it might not necessarily have been welcomed by all supporters as at least some would now have to spend much more time travelling across the city if they wished to keep watching the champions.

What appears to have angered the home fans was the feeling that many of the United players had not tried either to win the game or entertain them. People paid good money, which they had to work hard to earn, and if they were willing to spend it on football then the least they felt they deserved was 100 per cent effort from the players, even if the team they followed had won the League!

What sparked off the sustained abuse from the crowd was a remarkable incident just after half-time when no United player seemed keen to take a penalty they had been awarded. It had been expected that Sandy Turnbull would take the spot-kick but when he refused, citing later a couple of knocks to the head and a damaged ankle, Wall stepped forward to send the ball well wide and bring booing from the crowd. Writing in *The Football Field* the following Saturday the columnist 'the Mancunian' even reports that some of the Notts County players shook hands with Wall after he missed, which if true must give rise to the possibility that money had exchanged hands on the outcome of the match. This was to be the case seven years later when United played Liverpool in a relegation tussle and players from both sides won money by backing United to win 2–0.

As the game moved towards its conclusion it was apparent that a number of the United side were apparently indifferent as to how the game ended, and so when Notts County scored almost on full-time some spectators went absolutely wild and heaped further abuse on the side. George Dodd had taken the ball extremely well on the run and rounded Stacey before beating Broomfield with a low shot. There was some sympathy for the 'keeper in *The Manchester Evening News*. The paper's report said he did not deserve such hard luck and neither did the United defenders.

The hostility from the crowd was such that many of the United players took much longer than usual before deciding to leave the ground, by which time they would have become aware that with Manchester City and Sheffield Wednesday both losing, they were League champions.

The crowd's actions were subsequently the subject of much comment in many newspapers. One fan who wrote to *The Football Field*, signing himself 'Play Straight', had this to say: 'I am sure I am only voicing the opinion of 75 per cent of the spectators when I say that it was the most disgraceful exhibition of football that it has ever been my lot to witness between two teams. My complaint is purely and simply against the home team, who after the first 20 minutes never made an honest effort to score. 'Let the directors make a full and complete inquiry and if need be, get rid of the players who are to blame for I am sure the spectators would rather see a team of inferior men who played the game honestly than a lot of men who play ducks and drakes in a match.'

Other key fixtures
The Wednesday 1, Bolton Wanderers 2
Nottingham Forest 3, Man City 1

Manchester Cup semi-final

Date: Monday 13 April 1908

Result: Manchester United 3, Stockport County 1

Halse 3, Worth

United qualified for the Final after beating Stockport County in a fine semi-final in which Halse got a hat-trick, with Worth replying for County before a crowd of 8,000 at Hyde Road.

League Match 34

Against: Nottingham Forest (Away)

Date: Friday 17 April 1908

Attendance: 22,000

Result: Nottingham Forest 2, Manchester United 0

Nottingham Forest

Team: Linacre, Dudley, Maltby, Hughes, Wolfe, Armstrong, West, Marrison, Green, Morris, Spouncer.

Scorers: West, Marrison

Manchester United

Team: Broomfield, Stacey, Burgess, Duckworth, Roberts, Bell, Meredith, Halse, J. Turnbull, A. Turnbull, Wall.

For the second match running United lost to a side from Nottingham, but unlike the previous weekend when the players were roundly condemned for appearing not to try, Ernest Mangnall's side did, in fact, play well, especially in the first period when only a series of superb saves from the Forest 'keeper Harry Linacre and some poor shooting kept the score level. As half-time approached, Enoch West scored after being put through by Grenville Morris.

With Forest having lost only once at home all season, United were up against it in the second half, especially when West's clever pass saw Tom Marrison grab the home side's second goal. Despite the result, the home crowd gave the away team a great cheer at the end as a mark of respect for the new champions.

Enoch West

Finished as top League scorer with 28 goals at the end of the 1907–08 season, three ahead of Chelsea's Hilsdon and United's Sandy Turnbull, with Bache of Villa on 24 and Holley of Sunderland on 22. West was subsequently to sign for United at the start of the 1910–11 season, when with 19 League goals he helped the club carry off their second Championship title. In 1915 he was suspended for life for his part in fixing the Liverpool game on 2 April 1915.

League Match 35

Against: Manchester City (Away)

Date: Saturday 18 April 1908

Attendance: 40,000

Result: Manchester City 0, Manchester United 0

Manchester City

Team: Smith, Jackson, Norgrove, Buchan, Eadie, Blair, Webb, Thornley, Dorsett, Jones, Conlin.

Manchester United

Team: Broomfield, Duckworth, Stacey, Downie, Roberts, Bell, Meredith, Bannister, J. Turnbull, A. Turnbull, Wall.

Having suffered two consecutive defeats the champions would not have wanted a third, especially as they were playing Manchester City, whose previous day's exertions had seen them beat Birmingham 2–1. With Burgess out injured the United defence was reshuffled with Duckworth dropping to right full-back and Stacey moving across to the left to accommodate Downie at right-half. Bannister was back to partner ex-City man Meredith in place of Halse. With City winning the toss United were forced to kick against the wind, but they still made the first real chance of the game when Bannister split the home defence with a fine ball but Meredith, uncharacteristically, fired wide.

The Welshman's free-kick into the box then saw James Turnbull beat Walter Smith in the City goal, only to be left disappointed when the ball cannoned back into play off the upright. This was the start of some fierce United pressure during which the City team were forced to kick the ball desperately to safety and rarely threatened Broomfield in the United goal. Meredith seemed again certain to score but Jimmy Blair was in superbly to clear before the outside-right could line up his shot. Things got even worse for the home side when Bill Eadie, at centre-half, was so badly injured that he was forced to limp off the field. When he returned seven minutes later the cheers of the City faithful were rewarded with their side's first serious attack, but City were then back down to 10 within minutes, although thankfully Charlie Webb was soon back on the field. The two players were clearly not fully fit and in the second half spent much of their time together out on the right wing.

United were also handicapped by a player's injury, however. Heavily bandaged Sandy Turnbull had been so badly injured at Nottingham Forest that he really should not have played at Hyde Road. In essence the away side were playing with 10 men. Even so, James Turnbull should have given them the lead but his shot from just eight yards out was too close to Man of the Match Smith, who saved bravely. It was one of several fine saves by the City 'keeper. Despite having been largely outplayed the home side could have won the game when, with 10 minutes left, George Dorsett headed narrowly wide.

Although, as *The Manchester Courier* reported, there had been one or two 'incidents', it was felt that the 'play generally was in striking contrast to the first encounter earlier in the season at Clayton' when Sandy Turnbull had been sent off. The result kept City in with a chance of finishing in second place in the table behind their near neighbours. United, meanwhile, were in danger of failing to break the League record points total of 51 for a season and would require at least one win and a draw from their final three League games of the season.

League Match 36

Against: Aston Villa (Home)

Date: Monday 20 April 1908

Attendance: 10,000

Result: Manchester United 1, Aston Villa 2

Referee: H.S. Baslett of Gateshead.

Manchester United

Team: Broomfield, Duckworth, Stacey, Downie, Roberts, Bell, Meredith, Bannister, Picken, J. Turnbull, Wall.

Scorer: Picken

Aston Villa

Team: George, Lyons, Miles, Tranter, Logan, Codling, Wallace, Reeves, Hampton, Bache, Hall.

Scorer: Hall (2)

The counter attraction of the Manchester races kept the crowd to below 10,000 to watch a match played in bitterly cold conditions. After winning the toss Roberts forced the away side to kick into a stiff breeze in the first half and within a minute Billy George had to be down smartly to deny James Turnbull. Villa were ahead on three minutes after Alf Hall beat Duckworth with a lovely feint before hitting a shot that flashed just inside the post. It was a great goal. The League champions were level on 15 minutes, however, when Meredith's ball to Picken was knocked past George. Joe Bache threatened to restore the away side's lead as the game moved from one end of the pitch to the other.

Freddie Miles, not one noted for getting forward at the best of times for Villa, hit a long shot not far wide before Meredith struck his shot narrowly wide. United then suffered a blow when James Turnbull was badly injured, forcing him to limp out the rest of the game at outside-left. Just before half-time Hall should have made it 2–1 to Aston Villa but hit a low shot just wide of the post. The Villa forward was not to be denied, however, and in the second half he scored his second, and match winning goal, from the penalty spot.

Broomfield got his hands to the spot-kick but just failed to prevent the ball entering the net. With two goals Hall had been the man of a very fine match.

League Match 37

Against: Bolton Wanderers (Away)

Date: Wednesday 22 April 1908

Attendance: 18,000

Result: Bolton Wanderers 2, Manchester United 2

Bolton Wanderers ⚽⚽

Team: Davies, Slater, Stanley, Gaskell, Clifford, Boyd, Stokes, McClarence, Shepherd, White, McEwan.

Scorers: White, Shepherd

Manchester United ⚽⚽

Team: Broomfield, Duckworth, Stacey, Downie, Thomson, Bell, Meredith, Bannister, Halse, Picken, Wall.

Scorers: Halse, Stacey (pen)

Despite the fact that four goals were scored, this was a poor game. United, at least, had an excuse in that their side was badly disrupted due to injuries, and among some of those who did play there were some tired legs. Downie was retained at right-half, where he lined up alongside Ernest Thomson at centre-half, and there was second consecutive match for Picken.

This should have made it a perfect opportunity for near-neighbours Bolton Wanderers, who were desperate for points to stave off relegation.

Missing from the home side were key players in Harry Greenhalgh and Bert Baverstock, but they nevertheless had the advantage of opening the scoring on 13 minutes. The goal came after Duckworth could only breast an accurate Marshall McEwan corner away from the goalline and Wattie White was first to the ball to beat Broomfield from close in. Bolton were well in control, but just before half-time a blunder by Dai Davies saw Halse equalise after the United striker had shrugged off the Bolton half-backs.

Bolton were back in the lead in the first minute of the second half through Albert Shepherd, following up after Broomfield could only block a White shot, but again the home side failed from then on to press home their advantage and paid the penalty, literally, when Stacey converted one with 10 minutes remaining after Meredith had been brought down in the area by John Boyd. As a consequence the match ended 2–2, leaving Bolton needing a point against relegation rivals Notts County the following Saturday to guarantee Division One safety. United now needed to beat Preston North End on the same day to break Liverpool and Newcastle United's record points totals of 51 recorded in 1901 and 1907.

Footnote

Bolton's failure to go for a winner against United was compounded by losing 1–0 at home to Notts County in their final match. Notts County, who then by winning in midweek at Chelsea, courtesy of a highly debatable penalty, stayed up at The Trotters' expense. Bolton joined Birmingham in Division Two. Gaining promotion were Bradford City and Leicester Fosse. Both sides had finished well ahead of Wolverhampton Wanderers, who shocked everyone by beating the favourites Newcastle

United in the FA Cup Final. The match had finished 3–1 to the side from the Black Country, for whom the Revd Kenneth Hunt became the last amateur to score in a Cup Final.

League Match 38

Against: Preston (Home)

Date: Saturday 25 April 1908

Attendance: 8,000

Result: Manchester United 2, Preston 1

Manchester United

Team: Moger, Stacey, Hulme, Downie, Thomson, Bell, Meredith, Bannister, Halse, Picken, Wall.

Scorers: Own-goal, Halse

Preston

Team: McBride, Rodway, McFadyn, Lyon, McCall, McLean, Dawson, Wilson, Smith, Carlin, Bond.

Scorer: Lyon

There was a League debut for Aaron Hulme in the final League match of the 1907–08 season. With Downie and Thomson retaining their places at half-back the United fans were pleased to see Moger return to the side in goal after a number of weeks out with injury. Not that Broomfield had played badly, but Moger had performed with distinction throughout the season and was a fine 'keeper. With Sandy Turnbull still injured Picken retained his place in the side.

Preston North End were playing for pride, and were lying in 10th place at kick-off but with only three wins from 18 away fixtures.

There was a big cheer for Hulme when with his first touch in League football he headed clear as Dickie Bond shaped to head home a first-minute goal. Strong pressure from the home side then saw Wall hit the post before Charlie Dawson headed narrowly wide for Preston.

Billy Lyon, playing at right-half for Preston, found himself the object of the referee's displeasure shortly afterwards, a series of rough challenges earning him a booking after which he reacted childishly for some considerable period of the game, refusing to participate in the match or respond when the ball was played to him. His behaviour may have contributed to his side falling behind when after Billy Meredith broke through and shot Tommy Rodway turned the ball past his own 'keeper Peter McBride to make it 1–0 to United. Preston's 'keeper then kept his side in the contest with a fine save from Bell before a remarkable goal for the away side. Not that the shot was anything special. Moger might have stopped it on another day but it was special because Lyon had once again been persuaded to take part in the proceedings and with his first touch hit a free-kick into the United net. At half-time the score was 1–1.

When play resumed Wall and Thomson both had shots charged down, before Halse hit a piledriver that almost broke the crossbar, McBride doing his best to ensure he did not stand under it for the next few moments as it bounced up and down. The unlucky Halse was in scoring mood though and he headed home a Wall corner to make it 2–1, a result that would see the home side earn a new League points total of 52. Meredith might have made things safe but McBride was having a good game and was down well to smother the Welshman's shot. With neither side showing a great deal of interest in the last 15 minutes the game and the League season came to an end with a victory by two goals to one for the League champions.

The end of the game saw what were for the time some remarkable scenes. Around 1,000 fans congregated in front of the president's box for nearly an hour insisting upon the various players appearing at the window. It was a fitting end to a great League season, one all the players deserved as they had made history by becoming the first ever Manchester United side to win the First Division title and did so by establishing a record points total.

It would undoubtedly have been more if the side had been able to maintain their form of the first half of the season when they literally swept all before them, losing just a single game – at Middlesbrough – from the first 14 and winning at one point 10 in a row. This included one of the greatest performances ever by any Manchester United side when they thrashed the League champions Newcastle United 6–1 at St James' Park.

What undoubtedly held back United after the dawn of the New Year was the need to change the first team. Injuries and tiredness meant that whereas Ernest Mangnall needed to call on only 15 players for the first 20 of 42 League and FA Cup games during the season, 23 were used in the second half. There may also have been an element of complacency in the players' efforts when it became clear, after Newcastle had failed to avenge their earlier defeat in the return match at Bank Street in early February, that the title was as good as won and thoughts were turning towards the possibility of doing the League and FA Cup double.

That, of course, was to be foiled by a Fulham side that shocked the football world by beating the champions-elect in the quarter-finals in one of the greatest games ever played at Craven Cottage.

When the title was to all intents guaranteed at Everton on 8 April 1908 it followed a rousing last half an hour of play by Ernest Mangnall's men. After playing the hosts off the park, they had been stunned when Everton levelled but reacted by scoring almost immediately to restore the lead before winning 3–1 thanks to Wall's last-minute goal. This was one of 19 goals the outside-left contributed to the United Championship success, just six fewer than Sandy Turnbull. It meant the pair had contributed 44 of the side's 81 League goals. They, along with Billy Meredith, who continued to rip apart defences more than a decade and a half after he started playing professionally; Jimmy Bannister, who formed a deadly partnership with Meredith; and James Turnbull, with his boundless energy, dash and an eye for a goal, had forged a deadly front five that had torn defences to shreds.

They were able to do so because of the formidable half-back line up of Dick Duckworth; Alec Bell, quietly effective in everything he did; and the undoubted player of the 1907–08 season Charlie Roberts, whose passing to all areas of the field was unmatched by any player in the First Division that season. His heading, tackling and positional play was, to use a modern saying, out of this world.

Behind them they were fortunate to have in their side full-backs with real quality in Dick Holden and George Burgess initially and later George Stacey. In goal Harry Moger may never have been regarded highly enough by the England selectors to win an international cap but he was an excellent 'keeper who was brave, fast off his line and punched well. In an age where 'keepers could take a real battering he also gave as good as he got when facing opposing, often burly, forwards.

Good players, of course, do not always make great sides. For that to happen you also need a great manager, and it is to Ernest Mangnall's credit that he was able to fashion such a thrilling, winning side – one that can stand comparison with any Manchester United side that followed. Certainly Meredith, Roberts and Wall, and possibly Duckworth, would be strong contenders for inclusion in any all-time United XI. The Manchester United side of 1907–08 was clearly a great one and Mangnall's team, it must be said, made it possible for Manchester United to later become one of the world's greatest football clubs.

As a result of winning the League, United were invited to play in the inaugural FA Charity Shield match, which evolved from the Sheriff of London Charity Shield introduced at the end of the 1888–89 season as a professionals versus amateurs cup. When the latter fell out with the FA a new format in which the Football League winners played the winners of the Southern League was devised. United therefore played Queen's Park Rangers at Stamford Bridge.

FA Charity Shield ─────────────────────────

Date: Monday 27 April 1908
Against: QPR (Stamford Bridge)
Result: Manchester United 1, QPR 1

Manchester United

Team: Moger, Stacey, Burgess, Duckworth, Roberts, Bell, Meredith, Bannister, J. Turnbull, A. Turnbull, Wall.

Scorer: Meredith

QPR

Team: Shaw, MacDonald, Fidler, Lintott, J. McLean, Downing, Pentland, Cannon, Skilton, Gittons, Barnes.

Scorer: Cannon

This was certainly a game Manchester United should have won as they were the better side throughout the 90 minutes. They did, however, fall behind when early in the game Frank Cannon scored for the West London side. Meredith levelled the scores with a great goal when his shot from a tight angle completely beat Charlie Shaw in the QPR goal.

The Londoners were grateful to the 'keeper in the second period when he saved Stacey's penalty with a fine diving save. It was agreed to replay the match at the start of the following season, as United were unavailable for the rest of the season with games still to play at Newcastle and Manchester before taking part in a tour of Austria and Hungary.

Evelyn Lintott

Lintott was QPR's first-ever England international, making his debut against Ireland in Belfast in a 3–1 win in February 1908. In total he was to make seven appearances for his country, for whom he later laid down his life. He joined the British Army and became a lieutenant in the West Yorkshire Regiment and was killed in action on the first day of the Somme, 1 July 1916.

Fundraising match for Players' Union ————

Date: Wednesday 29 April 1908

Against: Wolves (St James' Park)

Result: Newcastle United 1, Manchester United 4

This fundraising match for the Players' Union drew a smaller than expected crowd following the home side's unexpected FA Cup Final defeat against Second Division Wolverhampton Wanderers. Those present saw the away side almost complete a similar scoreline as that back in October when Mangnall's men had won 6–1. In the event it was 'only' 4–1, with goals from Meredith, Sandy Turnbull, Wall and Roberts.

Manchester Cup Final ————

Date: Thursday 30 April 1908

Against: Bury (Hyde Road)

Result: Manchester United 1, Bury 0

Scorer: Bannister

After the game it was announced that all players had re-signed for the club except Bell and Broomfield.

Austro-Hungarian Tour 1908 ————

Following the season's end, the United board decided to reward the team with a trip to the Austro-Hungarian Empire. This took place only weeks before the national team made their first-ever overseas tour to play four matches against Austria, Hungary and Bohemia (as the Czech Republic was then called). Despite having won the League no Manchester United players were picked to play for England.

After arriving in Paris on Saturday 2 May United travelled on to Zurich, where on 6 May they played a combined Zurich XI, winning 4–2. Team: Moger, Duckworth, Stacey, Downie, Roberts, Bell, Meredith, Bannister, J. Turnbull, Picken, Wall.

On Saturday 9 May 1908 United beat SC Slavia 2–0 before a crowd of 5,000, with the goals coming from Picken and Bannister. Team: Moger, Duckworth, Stacey, Downie, Roberts, Bell, Meredith, Bannister, J. Turnbull, Picken, Wall.

On Sunday 10 May United again beat SC Slavia 2–0 before a crowd of 10,000, who saw Picken and Bannister again score the goals. Team: Moger, Stacey, Burgess, Downie, Roberts, Bell, Holden, Bannister, Duckworth, Picken, Wall.

On Wednesday 13 May United beat a Vienna XI side, consisting of players from Vienna SC, Vienna Athletic and Vienna FC, by four goals to nil in front of 2,000 people. The scorers were Turnbull (2), Picken and Wall. Team: Moger, Stacey, Burgess, Duckworth, Thomson, Downie, Meredith, Bannister, J. Turnbull, Picken, Wall.

On Friday 15 May United played Vienna SC, winning 5–0 with goals from Duckworth (2), Wall (2) and Turnbull. Team: Moger, Stacey, Burgess, Downie, Roberts, Bell, Meredith, Duckworth, J. Turnbull, Picken, Wall.

On 22 May they beat Magyar Athletikai 6–2 after leading 4–1 at half-time. Scorers for Manchester United were Picken (3), Wall, Thomson and Duckworth.

On Sunday 24 May the final game of the tour and the season sparked a minor diplomatic incident. It finished Ferencvaros Tornu 0 Manchester

United 7 with Bannister, Meredith (2), Wall (2), Picken and a penalty from goalkeeper Moger completing the rout.

There seems to be some doubt exactly what the cause was, but there was no doubt that abuse and more worryingly stones, in some cases of considerable size, were thrown at the players and a number were injured as a consequence, although none seriously.

Carrying a report from Reuters in Budapest, *The Manchester Guardian* on 26 May reported on 'the inability of the onlookers to appreciate differences between the rules obtaining in England and those which are recognized here.'

It was reported that the referee had wanted to send off three of the United side. There had been arguments over the use of goal judges stationed on the goalline, especially when they appeared to be shouting out to the referee what decisions to make. At one point Thomson appears to have grabbed hold of the referee, which the Reuters News Agency reported as an attempt to 'explain matters. In the discussion one or two of the visitors placed their hands persuasively on the referee's shoulder and the spectators in the cheap seats, misinterpreting the action, thought the Manchester men were trying to attack him. Considerable excitement resulted', but it does not appear from follow-up reports in the paper and in *The Manchester Courier* that at this point stones were thrown and that, in fact, when apologies were offered (by whom it is not certain from any of the reports) the match was restarted with all 22 players on the pitch.

However, after the match was finished some within the crowd, who were believed to have bet heavily on their side beating Manchester United, began throwing stones at the away players, and that at this point a body of mounted policemen came to their rescue and with swords drawn escorted them from the ground. However, after taking the players to what was felt to be a safe distance, and leaving them there, when the police dispersed more stones were hurled leading to the re-appearance of the police.

When peace was finally restored it was possible for both teams to attend the after-match dinner and the United side were accompanied to the station by their hosts, and it was reported that the First Division champions had agreed to play in Budapest the following year after the hosts offered their sincere apologies for the unfortunate events.

Whether this was really the intention we will never know. But by Friday morning (29 May 1908) when the side arrived back in London, but not until they had played a final game on 25 May against a mixed team drawn from Vienna clubs that was won 3–2, Ernest Mangnall had announced that while the club felt the tour had been a big success they would not be playing in 'Budapest or Slavia again'. In addition the United boss was reported in *The Manchester Courier* as saying that 'the idea of the foreign players seemed to be that all they do is to kick, push and hack. They go for the men and not the ball' and he finished by complaining about the standard of the refereeing.

When the side finally arrived back in Manchester, where Mangnall again described the tour as 'a big success, except for Budapest and Slavia', they were met with what the *Courier* described as 'a hearty welcome from a number of friends and supporters'.

FA Charity Shield Replay

Date: Saturday 29 August 1908

Against: QPR (Stamford Bridge)

Attendance: 6,000

Result: Manchester United 4, QPR 0

Manchester United

✪ ✪ ✪ ✪

Team: Moger, Stacey, Burgess, Duckworth, Roberts, Bell, Meredith, Bannister, J. Turnbull, Picken, Wall.

Scorers: J. Turnbull (3), Wall

QPR

Team: Shaw, MacDonald, Fidler, Lintott, J. McLean, Downing, McNaught, Cannon, Skilton, Gittons, Barnes.

In a match held over from the previous season United returned to the form they had exhibited in the first half of it, and QPR were fortunate not to suffer an embarrassing defeat. Special permission had to be given for the game to take place before the official starting date of the season, which was then 1 September, and a good number of newspapers were of the opinion that it should have been denied. These same papers were also critical of the decision of QPR not to play Fred Pentland, whom they had transferred to Middlesbrough during the summer, the feeling being that he should not have missed out playing in this most prestigious of events due to circumstances over which he had no control. Pentland later managed Athletico Madrid and Athletic Bilbao, taking the latter to two League titles and five Spanish Cups during the club's most successful period ever. Pentland still remains revered by the Basque supporters. His place in the replayed 1908 Charity Shield match was taken by John McNaught.

From the start Charlie Shaw was the busier 'keeper, punching clear a series of crosses before tipping over a beauty from Bannister. A last-gasp John MacDonald tackle then denied Picken; however, on 25 minutes Meredith got past Downing and James Turnbull turned his cross home to the cheers of the crowd, who clearly appreciated the style and panache of a United side in full flow. Ernest Mangnall's men were showing some superb skills with immaculate passing between the half-backs and forwards tearing QPR apart. Shaw rushed out to try to beat Turnbull to the ball but was only just too late.

Perhaps certain of their victory United then relaxed and might have paid for their complacency, but Alfred Gittons was unable to get round Stacey before Frank Cannon's shot was easily saved by Moger, back in the United goal after missing the original match in April.

On 56 minutes Wall made it 3–0, and just before the end of the game Turnbull completed his hat-trick to round off a thoroughly convincing 4–0 win that ensured United added another new trophy, the Charity Shield, to the Football League one they had captured for the first time at the end of the previous season. All they now had to do was win the FA Cup in 1909!

STATISTICS (competitive matches only)

Results

Date	Opponent	Competition	Result	Scorers
2/09/07	Aston Villa	(a) Division One	4–1	Meredith (2), Bannister, Wall
7/9/07	Liverpool	(h) Division One	4–0	A. Turnbull (3), Wall
9/9/07	Middlesbrough	(h) Division One	2–1	A. Turnbull (2)
14/9/07	Middlesbrough	(a) Division One	1–2	Bannister
21/9/07	Sheffield United	(h) Division One	2–1	A. Turnbull (2)
23/9/07	Manchester City	(a) Lancashire Senior Cup	3–0	A. Turnbull, J. Turnbull, Wall
28/9/07	Chelsea	(a) Division One	4–1	Meredith (2), A. Turnbull, Bannister
5/10/07	Nottingham Forest	(h) Division One	4–0	Bannister, J. Turnbull, Wall, og
12/10/07	Newcastle United	(a) Division One	6–1	Wall (2), Meredith, J. Turnbull, A. Turnbull, Roberts
14/10/07	Bolton	(h) Lancashire Senior Cup	2–0	J. Turnbull, A. Turnbull
19/10/07	Blackburn Rovers	(a) Division One	5–1	A. Turnbull (3), J. Turnbull (2)
26/10/07	Bolton Wanderers	(h) Division One	2–1	A. Turnbull, J. Turnbull
28/10/07	Oldham Athletic	(n) Lancashire Senior Cup semi-final	1–3	A. Turnbull
2/11/07	Birmingham	(a) Division One	4–3	Meredith (2), J. Turnbull, Wall

Date	Opponent	Competition	Result	Scorers
9/11/07	Everton	(h) Division One	4–3	Wall (2), Meredith, Roberts
16/11/07	Sunderland	(a) Division One	2–1	A. Turnbull (2)
23/11/07	Woolwich Arsenal	(h) Division One	4–2	A. Turnbull (4)
30/11/07	The Wednesday	(a) Division One	0–2	
7/12/07	Bristol City	(h) Division One	2–1	Wall (2)
14/12/07	Notts County	(a) Division One	1–1	Meredith
21/12/07	Manchester City	(h) Division One	3–1	A. Turnbull (2), Wall
25/12/07	Bury	(h) Division One	2–1	J. Turnbull, Meredith
28/12/07	PNE	(a) Division One	0–0	
1/1/08	Bury	(a) Division One	1–0	Wall
11/1/08	Blackpool	(h) FA Cup	3–1	Meredith, Wall (2)
18/1/08	Sheffield United	(a) Division One	0–2	
25/1/08	Chelsea	(h) Division One	1–0	J. Turnbull
1/2/08	Chelsea	(h) FA Cup	1–0	A. Turnbull
8/2/08	Newcastle United	(h) Division One	1–1	J. Turnbull
15/2/08	Blackburn Rovers	(h) Division One	1–2	A. Turnbull (pen)
22/2/08	Aston Villa	(a) FA Cup	2–0	A. Turnbull, Wall
29/2/08	Birmingham	(h) Division One	1–0	A. Turnbull
7/3/08	Fulham	(a) FA Cup	1–2	J. Turnbull
14/3/08	Sunderland	(h) Division One	3–0	Bell, Berry, Wall
18/3/08	Manchester City	(h) Manchester Cup	1–0	Wall (pen)

Date	Opponent	Competition	Result	Scorers
21/3/08	Woolwich Arsenal	(a) Division One	0–1	
25/3/08	Liverpool	(a) Division One	4–7	Wall (2), J. Turnbull, Bannister
28/3/08	The Wednesday	(h) Division One	4–1	Wall (2), Halse, A. Turnbull
4/4/08	Bristol City	(a) Division One	1–1	Wall
8/4/08	Everton	(a) Division One	3–1	Halse, Wall, A. Turnbull
11/4/08	Notts County	(h) Division One	0–1	
13/4/08	Stockport County	(n) Manchester Cup semi-final	3–1	Halse (3)
17/4/08	Nottingham Forest	(a) Division One	0–2	
18/4/08	Manchester City	(a) Division One	0–0	
20/4/08	Aston Villa	(h) Division One	1–2	Picken
22/4/08	Bolton Wanderers	(a) Division One	2–2	Halse, Stacey
25/4/08	PNE	(h) Division One	2–1	og, Halse
27/4/08	QPR	(n) Charity Shield	1–1	Meredith
30/4/08	Bury	(n) Manchester Cup Final	1–0	Bannister
29/8/08	QPR	(n) Charity Shield Replay	4–0	J. Turnbull (3), Wall

Final League Table (38 games played)

Team	Points
Manchester United	52
Aston Villa	43
Manchester City	43
Newcastle United	42
The Wednesday	42
Middlesbrough	41
Bury	39
Liverpool	38
Bristol City	36
Everton	36
PNE	36
Chelsea	36
Blackburn Rovers	36
Woolwich Arsenal	36
Sunderland	35
Sheffield United	35
Notts County	34
Bolton	33
Birmingham	30

League Goalscorers (81)

Alex 'Sandy' Turnbull	25
George Wall	18
James Turnbull	10
Billy Meredith	10
James Bannister	5
Harold Halse	4
Own-goals	3
Charlie Roberts	2
Jack Picken, William Berry, George Stacey, Alex Bell	1 each

League Appearances

Billy Meredith	37
James Bannister	36
George Wall	36
Richard Duckworth	36
Alex Bell	35
Charlie Roberts	32
Alex 'Sandy' Turnbull	29
Harry Moger	29
Herbert Burgess	27
Dick Holden	26
James Turnbull	26

George Stacey	18
Herbert Broomfield	9
Jack Picken	9
Alex Menzies	6
Harold Halse	6
Alex Downie	5
Ernest Thomson	3
William Berry	3
Aaron Hulme	1
Tommy Wilson	1
Kerr Whiteside	1
John McGillivray	1
Ted Dalton	1
Harry Williams	1